Keep Your Paws
on the Road

Published by Chew On This Publishing, LLC

Paperback ISBN-13: 978-0-9993057-0-6

Printed in the United States of America

Contents

Part 1

Travel Preparations

Training Exercises

Part 1

Contents

Part 2

On The Road

Training Exercises

Part 2

Dedication

We would like to dedicate this book to our dogs.
You have taught us a lot.
You have been patient with us.
You have brought us much joy.
You have been our loyal travel companions.

Introduction

by Birgit Walker

My husband, Jim, and I love to travel. There is so much to see and experience. We have been fortunate enough to see much of the world and have traveled to many different parts of the United States. Early on, we discovered that we missed our dogs when we traveled without them. We would be at a beach or on a hiking trail and one of us would say: *"I wish our dogs were here with us!"* - and the other would answer: *"I was just thinking about them. They would love this place."*

At restaurants, when someone had a dog with them, we'd go over and pet the dog. Then we'd tell the owner all about our dogs. Jim would look at me and say: *"I wish we had brought our dogs."*

Eventually, we decided to plan our vacations and weekend excursions with our dogs in mind. Well to tell the truth, at first we didn't plan. We just took our dogs. However, we soon learned that prior planning was required. Traveling with dogs was not as easy as it seemed. We found out that there are places our dogs can't go. We knew that finding a dog-friendly restaurant could be tricky, but we also ran into hiking trails that would not allow them.

Traveling with our dogs turned out to be a lot more work than traveling without them, but Jim and I agree, taking them along on our adventures is well worth it!

Some of my favorite memories include taking our dogs, Jaeger and Heidi, with us to Seattle, Washington. They went with us to Pike Place Market, one of the busiest places in downtown Seattle. Thousands of people were milling around the outdoor shopping areas. As we pushed our way through the crowded market, loud farmers and fishermen were hawking their goods. Jaeger, our 95 pound Chesapeake Bay Retriever, was walking close to my side. Heidi, our tiny Jack Russell Terrier, was safely tucked under Jim's arm. They might have preferred to be on the beach chasing a ball, but they were comfortable being with us no matter all the hustle and bustle around us.

In Montana, I fulfilled one of my dreams. Jim and I rented paddle boards and rode them down the Swan River near Flathead Lake. Jaeger and Heidi quickly accustomed themselves and I was able to ride with both dogs on my board. Something I had dreamed of doing for a long time!

Throughout all our travels, we meet a lot of other folks traveling with their pets. We often notice that many seem unprepared or poorly equipped. While talking with owners of dog-friendly accommodations, we found many of them had had bad experiences in the past with traveling pets. At some point we realized that there was a need for a book on traveling with pets. Not like one of the many others that may list dog-friendly restaurants or hotels and rates dog parks, but one that would provide helpful tips that would make traveling with pets easier.

As a dog trainer, Jim saw an opportunity to offer some simple training exercises. These are mostly behavior modifications that teach dogs to behave in a safe and agreeable manner.

The book you are now holding in your hands is the fruit of our many years of experience in training and traveling with our dogs. It is our hope that it will make your trips more enjoyable and that your dog will become a more comfortable, better travel companion for you.

Preface

by Jim Walker

I have been around dogs my entire life. Growing up in Kentucky, my family had dogs. In fact, my grandfather started the renowned Walker Hound breed. I can't remember ever being without a dog. They were my playmates as I swam and fished in the river.

When it came to choosing a career, I knew working with animals was what I wanted. My first job was at a racing stable in Kentucky. In 1984 I came out to Arizona and enrolled in Sun Valley Dog Training Academy, a dog trainer school. After I graduated, I moved to the San Diego area and found a job as a dog trainer with a kennel in Oceanside. A few years later, I took my sister's invitation and moved to the Big Island of Hawaii where I worked with the Humane Society. In 1990 I came back to Arizona to start my own business: a boarding kennel in Phoenix, Arizona.

Before I met my wife, Birgit, I worked 7 days a week boarding and training dogs. However, once we got married, Birgit taught me to relax and enjoy life a lot more.

Birgit is a very adventurous person who loves to travel. She introduced me to wonderful road trips and soon I took time off for weekend excursions and vacations. Almost every weekend we would load up the car and take our dogs somewhere in Arizona. Birgit would research and find places we had never been before. Sometimes we'd stay just for the day and return home that night. On other occasions, we'd spend several nights in a hotel or vacation rental with our dogs.

We always had the most fun on our trips when we took the dogs places that they enjoyed. We soon found ourselves planning our trips and vacations around them. Our dogs enjoy hiking and camping near lakes and creeks and hiking in and around waterways.

Once we started traveling with our Fifth Wheel, RV-ing became our favorite way to travel. We spend a lot of time in the wonderful National Forest areas of Arizona and nearby states.

Being a dog trainer, I often noticed varying levels of control other travelers had with their dogs. As we started across the country in our RV, we saw more and more people struggling with their dogs. Out of this came the idea of writing a book that would provide useful training tips for people who travel with dogs. It has always been my belief that dog owners enjoy taking their dogs more places when the dogs are well-behaved.

I hope that the information and training ideas we provide in this book will help many people enjoy taking their dogs with them on their weekend and vacation adventures.

How to Use This Book

This book is meant to be a guide for dog owners, who wish to take their dogs with them. Whether you travel far or just around the block, the information and exercises in this book will help prepare you and your dog.

As you read the book, choose the exercises and information that are useful to your specific situation. Practice is needed to train your dog - just reading and gaining an understanding will not change your dog's behavior.

Throughout the book, we have used the name "*Fido*" as we speak about a dog in general, and refer to the dog as male, using the pronouns *he* and *his*. This was done for simplicity only and is in no way meant to exclude female dogs. We know there are many wonderful female dogs out there ready to travel the world.

We divided the book into two parts. Part 1 offers training and information to prepare you and your dog. Read through these chapters and use the exercises and information to teach your dog these important behaviors.

The most important facet of traveling with your dog is to make sure he feels safe and comfortable. We have included information on how you can provide this security for your pet.

Preparing your dog for travel should be just as high of a priority as getting yourself ready for the trip. The information and exercises are designed to help alleviate stress and travel anxiety for both you and your pet. When you work with your dog, you form a bond, and your dog will learn to trust you. This obedience and trust will be invaluable as you venture out together.

There are numerous incidents where dogs run away or get lost on the road. This often stems from the dog being frightened, untrained, or out of control. The training exercises in Part 1 will help you teach your dog to trust and follow you on the leash into unfamiliar places, respect open doorways to keep him safe and learn to travel with you in your vehicle.

Part 2 of our book will provide you with helpful information on how to make your travel dog-friendly. You and your dog will learn to become a team ready for adventure. We have provided information on different forms of travel and helpful training tips to get your dog comfortable with these different modes of travel. Whether you take trips by car, boat, train or airplane, your dog needs to trust you to show him how to behave as you lead him into these new surroundings.

We have provided information on how to meet with other dogs, how to be a welcomed guest at dog-friendly accommodations, and how to teach your dog to come when called.

This book is not meant to teach a specific method or training technique. Rather, we provide general information that has worked for us and we deemed useful for dog owners traveling with their dogs. Every dog is different. You will need to experiment with your dog and choose the most effective approach. Since we cannot evaluate you, your dog, or the situation, the exercises and information are general in nature and are deemed appropriate for most people and dogs to practice. Every situation is different and depending on you and your dog, results may vary.

Throughout the book, we offer our FREE resources. These are available on our website at ModernCanineServices.com. We recommend you go to the website and watch some of our training videos. They will demonstrate many of the exercises mentioned throughout the book.

We offer suggestions for helpful training tools and give our personal recommendations on products that can be helpful for training or during your travel. These items may be available at local stores or other internet sites and it is your choice whether or where to purchase them.

Part 1

Travel

Preparations

Chapter 1

Training Guidelines

At home, you and your dog have a routine. It may not include taking him on walks around the neighborhood or to a local restaurant. You may not need to train him to respect an open doorway or walk on the leash without pulling. However, once you go on road trips, you will need to be able to walk with Fido on the leash a lot. Away from your usual and well-known surroundings, you will encounter a lot of different scenarios and your dog needs to respond consistently in a calm and obedient manner.

In the first part of this book, we share some of the behaviors and commands we deem essential for your dog to understand and follow while you are away from home. Essential commands are such that the dog's life could depend on him obeying in that instant.

Let's assume your dog is distracted by a squirrel causing him to chase after it. Offering a treat will likely not break that distraction. When you recall your dog, he will not be interested in the treat. The distraction of the squirrel is too much. The dog will ignore the treat and the command to come to you. On the other hand, if the dog is conditioned to obey your commands, he is likely to follow it even when there are distractions.

While treats are helpful with a lot of training efforts, they should not replace obedience. We use treats to teach basic commands or to redirect, but verbal praise and a pat on the head are our favorite ways to reward our dogs. We use treats to start our training in our backyard or inside our home, where distractions are minimal. We use the treat to show the correct behavior or teach a command. The dog responds to the treat because there is nothing else he would rather do. We remove the treat rewards as the dog progresses. Our goal in training is to have full voice control of our dogs.

How Dogs Learn

Dogs do not understand *"Don't do this."* Instead you must show your dog what it is you want him to do. Once a dog understands what it is you want, you need to condition him to consistently behave in the desired way. Over time with repeated training, your dog learns to behave in a new way.

You teach your dog by showing him the correct behavior following a command, but your dog will learn to do this behavior only by repetition. It is important that you understand that training your dog requires both teaching and conditioning.

For example, if you work with your dog on proper leash behavior and teach him that you want him to walk beside you on a loose leash, but then allow him to pull on the leash while on your regular walk, you are conditioning him to pull on the leash. You are being inconsistent in training him proper leash behavior. Only when you require him to behave in the same manner that you taught him in the training sessions will you see lasting results.

When your dog behaves in an unwanted way, you might be rewarding his behavior with your attention. For example, if your dog jumps on you and it is unwanted, ask yourself, *"What does he get from jumping?"* Maybe each time he jumps you give him attention. Know that even negative attention (you yelling at the dog) is giving him attention. Attention is a way to reinforce behavior. When you give attention to unwanted behavior, you unintentionally reward your dog for his action. With consistent repeated times of doing an activity, your dog will form a behavior. This is true for both wanted and unwanted behaviors.

To change his behavior, you must then replace the unwanted with the wanted behavior. You can discourage the unwanted behavior by ignoring it, or redirect the dog in some way. Your training is geared toward showing him the behavior you want.

Once your dog has learned the manner in which you want him to behave, expect it every time. That is consistency. If you have taught your dog to be quiet and calm when you put on his leash, don't allow him to jump around excitedly next time you are rushing to an appointment.

Birgit likes to do yoga each morning in our living room, or in the RV when we travel. Our dogs, Heidi and Jaeger, know to not interfere with her even though she is on the floor. When we got our new puppy, Apollo, he was not conditioned to stay out of her area during her yoga practice. Apollo would come and bring her toys, or rub against her, thinking she was on the floor to play with him. It took some time to teach him to stay away while Birgit was doing her yoga.

When Birgit talked to him or giggled, he would get even more persistent. Jim told Birgit to ignore Apollo, since talking was giving him attention. To show Apollo to stay out of her way, Jim told Birgit to gently push Apollo aside when he was in the way. If Apollo pawed at her when she was in a pose on the floor, Birgit would use a gentle

"*No*" and continue her practice. This was showing Apollo what was expected of him. As the puppy laid down nearby, Birgit would verbally praise him. This was enforcing the wanted behavior. It took only a few days for Apollo to learn that he was to stay out of Birgit's personal space when she was performing her yoga practice. Now, he simply lays down and sleeps or plays with a toy during her morning yoga practice.

Teachable Moments

Keep your training sessions short and focus on a particular behavior you want to improve. Your obedience training session should last no more than 30 minutes. Your dog's attention span will probably not last longer than that and your own patience may deplete shortly thereafter. You can even train him in short 10 or 15-minute sessions.

Training should always occur in a controlled environment. Choose an area based on what you want to teach. Make sure you have control of your dog by putting him on the leash. Train indoors or in a fenced in area. At first, a quiet area with no distractions is best. As training progresses, you can find areas with distractions to help you practice.

Set aside a short amount of time that you can devote to teaching your dog. Put yourself in the mindset of teaching with patience and equanimity. If you are already late for an appointment, don't try to train your dog not to bark excessively when the doorbell rings. Take 15 minutes in the evening when you are relaxed and create a teaching moment. Have your spouse ring the doorbell, while you are ready to address your dog's compulsive barking.

When you teach a new behavior, it is important to be patient with your dog. If you are rushed or frustrated, you should not train your dog. Go through exercises that show him what you expect, when you have time and can be patient. Conditioning occurs over time with repeated short training sessions.

To work on behavior modification, set up situations to work on. Don't get upset when your dog is showing unwanted behavior; rather, view this as an opportunity to teach. You cannot address a behavior unless you are right there when the unwanted behavior occurs. Therefore, it is important to set up situations in which the dog is first allowed to depict the undesired activity.

Always teach your dog by redirecting (move the focus of the unwanted or interrupt the unwanted) and then show the proper behavior. Over time, with consistency, the dog will be conditioned to act in the new desired manner.

For example: your dog is chewing up things around the house while you are out, how do you correct and redirect him? You need to create a teachable moment by getting him to chew on something he isn't supposed to when you are around to catch him doing it. You can leave things he usually likes to play with and chew on, scattered on your living room floor - shoes, socks, the TV-remote, or your children's toys for example. Stay close by and watch him. When he picks up one of the items he is not supposed to have, say the word "no" and clap your hands once. He will likely drop the item or at least look at you with the item in his mouth. Do not chase after him, as this would only make a fun game for him. Instead offer him something that he can chew on, like a nice soup bone you got from the butcher at the grocery store. In this way, you have interrupted the unwanted behavior with the "*no*" and the clap, and redirected him to the wanted behavior: the bone he should chew on.

Life is hectic and demanding. It's impossible to squeeze in dog training while rushing through your day. Consciously create teaching moments when you can be in control of your environment and your personal state of mind. Make the training sessions short but repeat them often. Be consistent in how you expect your dog to behave and most of all, always end on a good note!

Training Tools

Let us start by making sure you have the proper tools for training. In most exercises, we will ask you to use a leash and a collar. Below are descriptions of the training collar and leash we recommend. You can go to our website for more information on these training tools at ModernCanineServices.com. Go to our FREE resource tab to view training videos, where you can see Jim use these tools, or find them under our product recommendations.

The Leash

You want to get a simple six-foot leash. One end of the leash will have a clip that will attach to the collar. The other end will be a loop that you grasp with your hand. Choose a leash made out of leather or nylon.

Please do not use a retractable leash, a spongy leash, or any other leash for training as this may hinder the training process. Once your dog has learned proper leash behavior, you can use the retractable leash or other types of leashes during your regular walks. You should always use a standard, non-retractable leash when you train.

The Collar

The dog collar we recommend for training is a stainless steel slip collar. Unfortunately, this type of collar is also known as a choke collar. This name is very misleading and has a negative connotation.

When you shop at a pet store or online, look for a chain training collar, or martingale collar. If you ask for a training collar, you might be directed to an electronic collar or a pinch collar. Neither of these are what we want you to use here.

Be sure you get the right size training collar for your dog. It should have enough room to put your hand between the dog's neck and the chain. The training collar must fit loosely around the dog's neck and not be tight. Measure your dog's neck and add 2 inches. That will give you the right size for your training collar. From here on, we are going to use the term *training collar*.

It is best to use the training collar by itself. During your training sessions take off all other collars your dog wears. Outside of formal training, you can use any other type of dog collar. Switch back and forth if you currently use a different kind of collar. We are confident you will soon see the difference in your dog's behavior on the leash, and his responses to you, and will want to use the training collar more and more.

The training collar is our recommended tool for training, but the exercises and information can still be useful, even if you choose not to use it.

Calm Intent

During the training exercises, we ask you to speak very little to your dog. This is so that the energy during training remains calm. When your dog is overly excited, he will not be able to follow your direction or learn the new behavior. This is why we will always encourage you to get him into a calm and relaxed state first. To do this, you first must be calm and relaxed yourself.

Often behavior issues stem from dogs being in an overly excited state of mind. Many dog owners condition their dogs unintentionally to be excited. For example, a lot of dogs associate going for a walk with a hyper-excited state. They will jump around as soon as the leash appears. The owners interpret this behavior as the dog being happy to go outside. However, the excitement makes it very hard to put on the leash or walk out the door in a calm manner. Much of the excitement is caused by the owner talking to the dog in a happy, excited tone of voice. As humans, we communicate verbally first. However, canines and other animals communicate with body language first.

Whenever your dog displays such hyper excitement, you can help him get into a calmer state by not giving attention to him. Simply stand quietly until he calms down completely. Don't speak or touch him. Never pet your dog or praise him if he is in an overly excited state, as this only reinforces the excitement. Remain quiet and calm, relax and breathe. You will see your dog will calm down and sit or lay down. Your calm energy will calm him.

It is our overall intent to provide information and training exercises that will foster a bond between you and your pet. Dogs love to belong and have a strong sense of loyalty. When you interact with them in a way that has them learn to follow and trust you, they feel comfortable and secure. This is what we strive for because a dog that has formed this type of bond is a wonderful and reliable travel companion.

Chapter 2

Proper Leash Behavior

One of the most beneficial preparations is to train your dog to walk without pulling on the leash. You will have to walk your dog on a leash when you take him with you on day trips or vacations. You will walk him for exercise and allow him to relieve himself several times each day. This will be an uncomfortable chore if your dog does not know how to properly behave on-leash. Master this skill and you will greatly improve your travel experience with your dog.

You will likely encounter places with a lot of distractions: new smells, other dogs, and other people. It is important that you have control of your dog and that he trusts you to walk him through anything.

Many people walk their dog with the leash wrapped around their hands tightly, as their dog pulls them down the street.

Your goal should be to have your dog walk without any tension on the leash, calmly and without pulling or yanking. Your dog should never walk you. With the exercises in this chapter, you will start to teach your dog to follow you, not vice versa. This will form a bond and have him respect you as the one in charge.

Please always ensure your dog's safety by securing him with a leash before you go outside. You do not want him darting out of the door without a leash. We will cover respecting open doors in the next chapter, so for now, please be certain that you have control of the leash and that your dog is hooked up properly.

Start your leash training by selecting an area that has few or no distractions. Distractions can be children playing, other dogs being walked, and even other people. If possible, find an area that allows you to be undisturbed, just you and your dog. Use your six-foot leash and the training collar. At first, do the exercise outside your regular walks. During the exercise, you will not go very far, so exercise and allow your dog to relieve himself prior to the training session.

However, before you get started with Fido on the leash, we want to go over the best way to hold the leash, so you do not get hurt.

Grip the loop at the end of the leash with your dominant hand, with your thumb inside the loop, as shown in the picture below. Do not wrap the leash around your wrist, as it makes it very hard for you to switch hands and can be dangerous. A strong pulling dog can injure your wrist or shoulder.

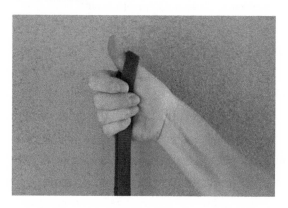

Control the length of the leash by running it through the other hand. Pick up any slack that is in the leash so that your dog does not get it wrapped underneath him. It may take some time to get this technique down. Take the time to practice it.

When walking your dog, hold your hand with the loop of the leash close to your body. We are not kidding when we say your dog could pull your arm out of your socket when he pulls to the end of the leash.

Leash Training

The following exercises will help you train your dog to walk on the leash without pulling. Since you are training your dog to never pull on the leash, you do not need to have a command.

In the quiet area, you selected for the exercise, choose two focal points for yourself. A parked car and a tree, or a mailbox and a street lamp. These two points should be about 100 feet apart. From here on out we will refer to them as marker A and marker B. It is important to keep moving during the exercise, so do not stop walking.

Leash Training Exercise

To start the exercise, walk slowly toward marker A. Your dog will likely be in front of you pulling on the leash. That's okay, just keep walking toward A. Once you get to the marker, turn your focus on your second marker and start walking towards B. Your dog, thinking he knows where you are going, will be pulling you towards B, or maybe he is pulling towards somewhere else he wants to go sniff. Let him go to the very end of the six-foot leash and as soon as the leash gets tight, turn 180 degrees and walk back towards A.

It is very important that you continue to walk. Do not stop or try to call your dog towards you. Just walk back toward A. The training collar will do all the work. Your dog will hear the zipping noise and feel the collar tightening. Your movement into the opposite direction will get him to turn and look. He will see your backside as you are walking back toward A. In his mind, he wants to get out in front of you, so he will dart past you and pull toward point A. Just as soon as he runs past you and the leash gets tight, turn again 180 degrees and start to walk towards B. Do not stop and don't say anything. Just walk towards B.

Each time your dog gets to the end of the leash and pulls, you change direction. By doing so, the training collar will make the zip noise and then get tight. Your dog will want to relieve the pressure. Within a few times, he will associate the zip noise with collar tightening, so he will react prior to the leash getting tight. As long as the leash is loose, continue to walk forward. As soon as your dog pulls on the leash, change direction. Remember that you are not out going for a walk. You are training your dog to follow you.

Continue to do this exercise until you notice that your dog is watching you closely. As soon he gets it, he will stay close to you and watch where you are walking.

The most important thing for you to do is to continue to walk. It may take him a few minutes to figure out what is going on. Pretty soon he will start to catch on and will stop running past you to get in front. He will realize that as soon as he zips past you, you will change your mind and go in the other direction. He will learn that he needs to pay attention to you and will stay closer to you.

At first, he will start to look back over his shoulder to make sure you are still going in his direction. Soon he will stay close by your side, so he can keep an eye on you.

When he pays attention to you, start making turns more frequently, even if he isn't pulling. You are looking for him to turn around as soon as you make that 180-degree turn. When he makes this choice to keep an eye on you and follow you, start to praise him.

You may say, "good dog!" but do not stop to pet him. Continue walking.

Praise him when he's paying attention to you and not pulling on the leash. Make your 180-degree turn if he walks past you and pulls on the leash.

Remember the difference between teaching and conditioning. Teaching means you are showing your dog what you want him to do. That is what you are doing with this exercise.

Conditioning means to consistently expect the learned behavior so it can become a habit. You both need conditioning. You are learning the proper way to walk your dog and your dog is learning that it is not acceptable to pull on the leash. He is learning that you will not tolerate pulling on the leash because it's unpleasant. He is learning he must pay close attention to you in order to keep up with his crazy owner who keeps changing directions.

As you read through this, you may not immediately understand why this will work, but you will soon see the improvement in your dog's behavior on the leash during the exercise.

Let us cover some of the things that you may encounter while training with this exercise.

1. You may think that your dog should stop pulling on the leash the very first time that you make your 180-degree turn. He won't and it's okay. More than likely, he will run past you and hit the end of the leash before you even complete your turn. Don't give up. Just turn as soon as you can. Stay calm, breathe and do not talk to him. The most important thing for you to do is to just keep moving. You don't have to move fast. Just don't stop. Simply walk at a regular speed and make your 180 degree turns slowly. The gentle tug that happens

automatically when you walk in the opposite direction is correcting the unwanted behavior of pulling on the leash.

2. You may have the urge to stop walking when he is behind you pulling in the opposite direction. Don't stop, just keep walking forward. He has to see you moving when he turns around to look at you. If you are standing still when he turns around to look at you, he will continue to try to get you to move in his direction. Most of the time people will have a hard time walking in a straight line. They will end up walking in a circle trying to keep an eye on their dog. This is why we use our two points for this exercise. Keep your eyes on your landmarks and walk between point A and point B. Don't look at your dog, just keep walking.

3. It does not matter which side he passes you on or where he wants to pull you. Don't get frustrated and don't say anything to him. Just stay calm and continue to switch direction between the two landmarks whenever the leash gets tight.

To see this exercise performed, you can go to our website and look for the FREE resource tap. We have several short training videos on our YouTube channel that show this technique. Our website is at ModernCanineServices.com.

Continue to practice until you see a measurable improvement. It should only take a few of these training sessions to make a big difference in his behavior on-leash. After a few sessions, he should walk without pulling on the leash and stay close to you. Now you should expect this kind of behavior on your regular walks from this time forward. He has learned the proper behavior you expect, now it's time to condition him to do it! Require him to walk on a loose leash and correct him when he is pulling.

Work with Distractions

Now that you have taught your dog what you expect on-leash, expect the same loose leash in all situations.

Let's say a person with another dog is 50 yards away and your dog starts to pull towards them. As soon as the leash gets tight, make your 180-degree turn away from the distraction. Remember the most important thing is to keep on walking. Don't say anything. Change directions and expect him to follow you. Increase distance until you get him back under control. If he is not calming down, take him away from the distraction. Don't get upset or frustrated. View these instances as training opportunities.

Continue with your 10-15 minute daily training sessions by looking for distractions to practice with. Go past homes that have a dog behind a fence. Practice walking past without him paying attention to the dog barking or jumping on the fence. You will soon see that your dog will become more conditioned to walk on a loose leash for you.

Once your dog walks on the leash without pulling, you will enjoy your walks much more. Many of our clients tell us that this training has improved their travels in many ways.

Chapter 3

Wait for Safety

Your dog should never run out of an open doorway. Think about the consequences. As you travel with your pet, you will be in unfamiliar surroundings. If your dog runs out of the open car door or hotel room door, he can easily be lost or injured.

Similar to leash training, you won't teach a command, you will instill a behavior that will be regularly expected. We can't think of another training that we deem more important to teach than this one.

You already know your dog's current behavior. What happens when you open the door to the outside world? Does your dog sit or stand quietly looking to you for direction? Or does he just run through the door as soon as it is opened? Maybe he even gets super excited and jumps around the door as soon as anyone approaches it.

If your dog does anything other than wait to be told to go through the doorway after you, you need to practice the exercises in this chapter! Your dog should never charge the front door when you open it. Whether you leave and he has to stay behind, or you open the door to let someone in. Even when you take him for his walk.

In general, there is no need for a command to tell him not to charge the door because it is a behavior you expect from the dog at all times. You simply have to teach him and condition him to do this consistently.

Our first exercise will have you teach the dog to wait for you to walk through the door when you take him outside for his daily walks. Practice at the door you go through regularly for your walks together.

Start with a Calm Dog

Make sure your dog is calm. For many dogs, the leash brings a lot of excitement. They get so happy they can hardly contain themselves. If this is the case for your Fido, make sure you don't put the leash on right by the doorway and don't say anything. Many dog owners unintentionally add to the hyper excitement by happily asking their dogs: *"Do you want to go on a walk?"*

If your dog is already associating an excited state with the leash, make it a regular habit to pick up the leash throughout the day, when you don't plan to go for a walk. This will help desensitize your dog, and teach him to associate the leash with a calm state of mind. Simply walk around with the leash in hand and ignore your dog. Please do not say anything to him. Just hold the leash for a few minutes and then put it back down. Repeat several times a day.

When you are ready for the exercise, attach his leash to his collar away from the front door. Stand quietly and still for a few moments. Your dog will calm down and eventually just look at you for guidance. Wait until he is completely calm before you do the exercise.

Door Exercise 1 – Going for a Walk

Walk toward the front door and expect your dog not to pull on the leash. Just as in the previous chapter, change directions and walk away from the door if your dog is pulling toward it. This is very similar to the original leash training exercise in Chapter 2 - (marker A is the door to the outside and marker B is the other direction, back into the room).

Continue to walk toward the door as long as your dog is calm and walks next to you on a loose leash. Immediately turn and walk back into the room if he pulls on the leash. It is imperative that you not talk. Make sure you are calm and relaxed. If you are frustrated, your dog will pick up on your state of mind. Walk back and forth until he quietly walks next to you toward the door.

Now that he is quietly standing next to you by the door, open it a little. Ideally, he will just wait for you to open the door and walk through with you on a loose leash. If he starts to squeeze through the half-open door or pulls you through the door once it is open, tell him *"No,"* followed by closing the door. Walk back into the room.

Open the door only slightly and gently close it if he tries to squeeze through. You may need to open the door a few inches and close it right before he can get his nose into the crack. Make sure the leash is slack. Do not pull him back, let him back up himself.

Repeat until he waits quietly for you to open the doorway.

Next, practice with the door wide open. With your dog securely on his leash and collar, open your front door all the way and from the inside walk toward the open door. If he pulls on the leash, say *"no"* and change direction. Simply walk back into the room. Turn and walk back toward the open door. Repeat as needed until you can reach the open door with the dog on a loose leash.

Stop right by the doorway and do not allow your dog to go through it. Praise him verbally for being calm and quiet, but do not pet him. If you bend down to pet, he will likely get excited and you may lose some of the calmness you have worked so hard to get.

Now you can invite him to follow you through the doorway. Once he follows you calmly through the doorway make him stop and wait while you close the door.

If he rushes past you and gets through the door, do not pull or yank him back. Simply turn and walk back into the house. Remember the exercise in leash training. You want him to pay attention to you and follow you.

Repeat the exercise several times. Expect this behavior every time you take him for his walk from now on. It may take a little longer to get through the door in the first few days, but he will soon be conditioned to behave in this manner. Do the same for other doors. For example, use the same exercise to enter and exit the dog park or the backyard gate.

Respect the Open Door

With this next exercise, you will train your dog to stay away from the door when you leave or when someone comes in. You will not use the leash and collar for this exercise.

Decide on an acceptable distance away from the door for him to be when you want to open your door. You may wish to find a visual marker that shows you the distance. You should make this no less than six feet away from the doorway. Have an imaginary six foot half circle around the doorway where your dog is not allowed.

Since he is not secured by the leash, make sure you are controlling the situation and are comfortable you will be able to close the door before the dog could dart outside. If you are not comfortable with this, you can put the leash on him and let it just drag on the floor. This will give you the opportunity to step on the leash if he runs past you.

There is no reason to swing the door open wide. Just open it a little bit at a time.

Door Exercise 2 – Respect the Open Door

Walk up to the door that you are going to use to teach him. When he walks up to the door with you, he will probably have his nose on the door waiting for you to open it. You will step between his nose and the door and walk into him until he backs away from the door. Use a tall upright posture, using the front of your legs to gently walk into his space. The dog will back up. You can have your hands down by your side and palms forward.

The key is to stay calm. There is no need to talk or to scold him. Use your command only once. For example, you might use *"Back,"* *"Back up,"* or *"Stay back."*

Do not reach for the dog or use your hands to grab or push your him away. Use your entire body to get him to back up. As he is backing, you will want to "steer" him into the direction that you want him to go. Continue to walk into him until he backs up the acceptable distance away from the door. Once he is far enough away, stop and just stand there for a moment. He should be looking up at you for guidance. You can tell him he is a good boy, or tell him to stay. Preferably, he will relax and either sit or lay down.

If he walks around you, just continue to herd him back in the same manner as described above.

Now walk back to the door and he will probably follow you again because that is what he has always done. Turn around and walk into his space until he starts to back up again. Continue backing him up until he is again back in the space that you want him to be.

After your dog is in his space, walk to the door and put your hand on the door knob. Have your back toward the dog. If he remains in his place, gently open the door a few inches. Just open it a little. There is no need to fling it all the way open at this stage in the training exercise.

Just as soon as Fido approaches the door, say *"No"* and close it immediately. Start to walk into your dog's space again until he backs up. When he is in his place outside the imaginary circle, go to the door and try and open it again.

Anytime during the exercise, if he approaches the door, say *"No,"* close the door and herd him back.

Stay consistent. Your dog will begin to understand what you want from him. How fast this exercise goes is not important. Do not open the door until he stays in his space, away from the door.

Use verbal commands and encouragement as you do the exercise. For instance, use the command *"Get back"* while herding the dog to the proper distance. Remain calm and use a gentle tone of voice. Say the command once, don't repeat it several times as you walk into him. When he reaches the area you want him to remain, say *"Good dog,"* but don't touch him. Give a treat if you like. Tell him, *"Stay."* If he walks around you, step in front of him and say *"No."* Walk into him until he backs up again.

Do this until you are able to open and close the door without him approaching the door. Once your dog remains in his place while you open and close the door, get another person in the household to do the same. Include any children old enough to understand what you are doing.

If you have multiple pets, we highly recommend you do the exercise with each one separately. Once each pet understands where you expect them to be, you can practice with the whole gang.

Decide what you expect your dog to do when you leave the house or someone is coming into your home.

For example, you can teach your dog to lay down on his bed while you greet your guests. You tell your dog to *"Lay down"* and point toward the mat. He is expected to go over to his bed and remain there until he is released. After your guests are inside the house, you can release your dog from his stay on his bed. We use *"Take a break"* for our dogs. You can use any command you would like, just as long as you are consistent. Some people use the word "*OK*" as their release command. We would caution against it. Imagine you have your dog in a "*stay*" and someone asks you how you are doing. If you say "*OK*," your dog will likely hear it as his release to get up.

If you decide to put your dog in his spot when you leave home, use a different command. The command "*Stay,*" requires a release command. You do not use the *"Stay"* in this scenario because you do not wish for him to remain on his bed for the entire time you are away from home. Tell him to *"Lay down."* Now he can go to his spot and stay there until you leave the house. Closing the door is his release command.

Respect Car Doors

Whenever you travel with your dog in a car, it is equally important to teach him to wait until you tell him it is safe to come out. This can literally be a life saver! We have heard of many tragic stories where dogs have been injured or killed when they jumped out of the car and into traffic.

It is important that you have done the proceeding door exercises with Fido, as you have no way to walk your dog in the opposite direction in the car. Your dog should already know that an open door does not mean he can rush out. You are just showing him that the same applies to car doors.

We use a hand command in addition to the verbal *"stay"* command. It can be very noisy on the roadways and rest-stop areas at times. Having the additional hand signal helps the dog focus on the handler.

Chapter 6 offers an exercise to teach your dog to respect the car door. To see the exercise performed by one of our dog training clients, you can visit our FREE resource tab through our website under training videos at ModernCanineServices.com.

Chapter 4

Crate Training

In this chapter, you will get your pet acclimated to spend time in a crate. Being able to put your dog into a crate is a must, especially when you travel by airplane, but is often required while staying in a hotel room or vacation rental. Crate training is also useful in housebreaking, car travel, and in situations where the dog will be unattended. It is also a great tool to help dogs with separation anxiety. We recommend that all dogs are accustomed to being in a crate.

Jim's sister adopted a Cairn Terrier mix from the local Humane Society. She named her Pua. Pua had been adopted and returned 3 times because she had separation anxiety. If left alone at home, Pua would destroy furnishings and carpeting. If left in a crate, Pua would panic and destroy everything in the crate and try to escape the crate. She even chewed through the plastic bottom of a wire crate. Jim helped his sister and her husband to crate train Pua with the exercises in this chapter. They patiently worked with her on becoming comfortable in the crate, and were able to leave her inside when they left the home. This taught Pua to be comfortable with being left alone.

Today, Pua shows no more signs of destructive behavior when she is left home alone, or by herself in the RV, even without a crate.

Getting your pet used to the crate is not difficult, it just takes time, consistency, and patience. It is very important that you view the use of the crate as a positive place for your pet. Use of a crate must never be punishment or anything negative. If your pet perceives the crate as punishment, your pet will not enjoy staying in the crate and will resist going in every time.

You will teach your pet that the crate is a safe and secure place to be. It can be your pet's personal private space.

This chapter is very detailed. It was written for dogs like Pua, who are afraid to go into the crate or for dogs who have not been in a crate. You may not need all of this information. We don't know your situation, so we have provided the training in great detail. Use what you need and skip over the parts your dog is comfortable with. If your dog is uncomfortable with the crate or has never had experience with it, we strongly recommend you skip the crate assessment exercise. Go directly to the step-by-step training provided.

The Crate

When it comes to crates, there are a lot of different choices for you. In general, purchase a crate that will be large enough for your adult dog to stand up in with some room to spare, and room for him to be able to turn around. It is always best to purchase one size larger, rather than to have one that is too small.

When you purchase his crate, think about when and where you will use it. If there is any chance you will use the crate to travel with your dog by airplane, be sure to get one that is airline approved. (More on this in Chapter 14.) To see our product recommendations visit our website at ModernCanineServices.com.

Crate Assessment

Maybe you feel your dog is comfortable in the crate and is ready to travel, or you may not know for sure. Run through the following crate assessment exercises to find out, if he is truly ready, or where to start his training.

The assessment will show you if your dog is already familiar and comfortable with the crate. Many people use the crate, but their dog is not comfortable in it. This usually results in the dog barking or whining when left in the crate for longer periods of time. In extreme cases, the dog will destroy the bedding inside the crate or try to escape it. If you already know from experience that your pet resists being in the crate, skip the assessment exercise. Go right to the next part and start with the first crate training exercise.

Crate Assessment Exercises

1. With the door wide open, toss a toy or treat into the far back of the crate and let your dog retrieve it.

Did your dog go in without hesitation?
Did he seem to want to hurry back out quickly?

If your dog is hesitant and locks up his legs and does not want to go in, you have a very good indication that you should go through all the step-by-step training in this chapter. Don't force the issue by pushing him into the crate. Quit the assessment and start the crate training process.

2. Place another treat into the far end of the crate. This time, gently close the door once your dog goes to retrieve it. Stand right in

front of the closed door, so the dog can see you. Observe your dogs behavior, but do not speak to him.

Did your dog seem relaxed?
Was your dog whining or barking at the door to get out?
Did your dog eventually sit or lay down and wait patiently?

Within a few minutes, your pet should lay down and relax. If he is quiet after 3 minutes but is still not laying down and relaxing, give him more time. He has not made a decision on what action to take.

If he isn't laying down or he is whining or trying to get out, open the crate without any words. You don't want to give him any positive attention for not wanting to be inside the crate. End the assessment and go to the step-by-step exercises in this chapter.

3. If your dog is relaxed in the crate with the door closed, leave the room, so the dog cannot see you anymore.

Did your dog lay down patiently?
Did he bark or whine?
Did he scratch at the door trying to get out?

All you're doing here is making sure he will remain quiet in the kennel after he no longer sees you. If he remains calm and quiet, *congratulations*, your dog is comfortable and will likely not need any further training on the crate.

If your pet barks while he is in the crate and does not choose to lay down and relax, you should go through this chapter and work through the exercises. The following exercises will help him understand that the area he is confined in is his safe place and that you will return for him later.

End the assessment, by opening the crate without any words, so to not encourage his not wanting to be in it.

Crate Set-up for Training

Find a place to set up the crate inside your home. Part of the training will have Fido spend time inside the crate. We recommend you set it up near a chair that you can sit in. For example, you can have the crate in your living room next to your TV chair. Maybe you can have it in your office by your desk area, so you can practice while you work on your computer. Please don't put the crate in a far away corner of your home. It needs to be in a place where the dog can see you and other family members.

It is best to set the crate in such a way that it does not make a lot of noise when the dog gets into it. If the crate is placed on a hard floor, such as tile, it can rattle and scare an insecure dog. We recommend you place it on a carpeted area or put a blanket or piece of carpet underneath it. Some weight on top of the crate helps keep it quiet when your dog goes in and out. Crate movements or noises can often be a big scary factor in the beginning of the crate training. Books or other heavy items on top of the crate will ensure it is firmly pushed to the ground. Test it by grabbing the front by the door and slightly wiggle it; make sure the crate does not move or make scary noises.

To make it a comfortable place to rest put his dog blanket or dog bed inside. Do not put a water bowl inside as that will just lead to a mess. However, place one or two of his favorite toys inside. The smell and familiarity of bedding and toys will signal your dog this is where he is supposed to hang out or sleep.

Crate Training

This first section is for the dogs who absolutely want nothing to do with the crate. If your dog will not go into the crate after a treat and panics when you close the door, you want to start with these exercises. Don't worry about why he is apprehensive. Whatever has happened in the past with your dog is in the past. You will start now with conditioning your dog to see the crate as his own little domain.

Follow this section from the very beginning and do not move on until you see your pet is completely comfortable with that stage of training. Repeat the exercise as often as needed. Give your dog all the time and patience needed with this training. Do not hurry along or skip any exercises.

For sensitive dogs, you don't want the door accidentally closing on your pet. Remove the door for the first few exercises.

With his favorite bedding inside the crate, weighted down so it doesn't make noises when your dog goes in, and the door off, it's time to get started.

Find a high-value treat. Something you know your dog loves. Small size treats are best, as you will use several treats to get your dog comfortable with walking in and out of the crate.

For this exercise, you want the dog to walk into the crate without pushing or leading him. You are using the treat to entice him to go inside.

We caution you, do not physically touch your dog at the moment he is eating the treats or he might be afraid that you are going to force him into the crate. You may lose a lot of conditioning that you have gained. However, give him lots of calm verbal praise and encouragement. Be aware of the energy level you are projecting. You must remain calm, not excited and loud.

Remove Fear of the Crate

Put one of your dog's favorite treats in front of the crate on the floor. Not inside, but in front of it. Encourage your pet to eat the treat. If your dog eats the treat and he does not look at the crate, you are off to a good start. If your dog is afraid to eat the treat because the crate is nearby, move the treat further away from the crate until your pet eats the treat.

Once the dog eats his first treat, move the next one closer to the crate. If he does not eat that treat because he is afraid of the crate, don't panic. Encourage him to the treat. If he remains hesitant, simply leave the treat and walk away. Because he has already eaten a treat and the crate did not hurt him, he will want this one. It might take a few minutes but he will eat that treat. Give him time and don't force the issue. Allow him to do it on his own. Don't try to coax him to come closer. Just leave the area. You can check back within a few minutes. Continue with the training exercise when the treat is gone.

Decrease the distance to the crate by half every time until you can place treats right in front of the open crate.

When your dog is not concerned about the crate any longer, you can put the next treat right inside. Do not move too far into the crate. Make sure his feet can still stay outside of it at first. If at any time he hesitates and won't go after the next treat, just leave it and walk away. Let him work through this on his own.

Into the Crate

You guessed it, next, place the treat just far enough in so that he has to put both front feet in the crate to reach it. This will probably be the hardest one for your dog to do, but when he conquers this, you're almost home free. Don't rush ahead! If he steps in but rushes back out without the treat, give him time to investigate and let the treat sit there tempting him. He could be full and not interested in the treat now. Just go about your day and every once in awhile check to see if the treat is still there.

When he is comfortable with his head and front feet in the crate, go half the distance again to the back and add another treat that will cause him to have all 4 feet inside. If he is concerned about it that's okay. Leave it there and let him work through it just like in the previous stages.

To finish this exercise you should be able to throw a treat to the back of the crate and your dog will go in, grab the treat, and come back out without much concern. Make this a regular exercise for a few days.

These first two exercises are for dogs that are frightened of the crate. Your dog may go in and out quickly or it may take several days to get him to associate the crate with a fun place to find treats. Make sure you pay close attention to your dog's body language and give him the time he needs to form this very important first impression.

Feed Inside the Crate

Once he is comfortable going in and out to retrieve his treats, the next step is to have him stay inside for short amounts of time. This helps build the foundation of comfort in the crate.

For this purpose, you can feed your dog daily in the crate. Leave the water outside, as it will just cause a mess.

Place just a small amount of food inside his dog bowl. This will make it easier to notice if he has been eating or not. You can start this process by placing his dog bowl in front of the crate. If he does not eat when you first put the bowl down, don't worry. It might mean that he is just not hungry. Leave the bowl there and go about your business. You can check on the bowl every now and then. Just like the previous exercises, move the bowl inside the crate a little at a time.

Every time you fill up the bowl, move it deeper inside, until the bowl is in the very back and he is able to go in and eat without much concern. This will be the only place for a while that you will feed him. Do not worry that your dog will starve, just move the dog bowl closer to the door until he eats some food. It is really up to your dog how long this exercise will take. The goal is to have him comfortably eating in the back of the crate with all four feet inside the crate. Continue feeding him back there for several days.

Stay Inside the Crate

If you took off the door of the crate for the previous exercises, make sure you reattach it for the next step.

The crate should be placed so that the dog can see you from the inside of the crate, sitting in your chair. Place his favorite toys inside.

You will want to start using a command to tell your dog that you want him to go into the crate. We use *"Kennel up,"* but you can use anything you want. Make sure you use your command from now on every time you want your dog to go into the crate.

In this first exercise, you will teach your dog to go into the crate on command and then stay calmly inside until you tell him to come back out. At first, you will only ask him to go inside and then let him come back out. Later you will extend the time he spends inside.

Teach him that you can open the door to the crate and he won't charge out. This is similar to the front door exercise you used in Chapter 3.

You may be tempted to replace a toy for the treat. However, retrieving a toy encourages the dog to go in and come right back out. Use the treat, as you want the dog to stay inside the crate until you invite him back out.

Stay in the Crate

Use your command and toss the treat into the back of the crate. Your dog should go in after the treat. After he goes inside, quietly close the door behind him.

Stand right in front of the crate and tell your dog *"Good dog."* Wait just one moment. Your dog should be standing there looking at you. Tell him to stay. Say: *"Good dog. Stay."*

Now slowly open the door to the crate a little. If he tries to push out, gently close the door and say *"No. You stay."* Gently open the door again. Close it if the dog wants to push out, but this time do not say anything. Continue to open and close until your dog steps back or sits down. He will look to you for guidance.

When he no longer tries to push through, open the door and give a command to come out.

Continue the above to teach the command to go into the crate. Teach him to patiently wait until he is invited out. You can now start to increase the time he is inside. Put him inside and sit nearby in your chair to watch TV, read a book, or work on your computer. For now, it is important that you remain in his sight. Let him be sure you are nearby.

Over the next few days, have repeated sessions with your dog in the crate, with you nearby. Plan on him spending some time in the crate every day. Slowly increase the time span. Watch the news or read a few chapters in a book.

The next exercise teaches you what to do when your dog starts to bark or whine for attention. You will learn to teach him to be quiet while he is inside.

Before you start with the next exercise, make sure that he has had a good amount of physical exercise prior to the crate time and has had an opportunity to relieve himself.

Correct Barking or Whining for Attention

Put him in the crate as usual. You'll want to sit down in your chair and relax. If he just stands and looks at you but is quiet, you can praise him.

You might be tempted to try to console your dog when he starts whining, but that only encourages more of the same behavior. He is whining because he wants your attention. When you talk to him, you're unintentionally reinforcing the behavior that you don't want. So when he whines, continue to watch the TV, or read your book. Ignore your dog's whine.

If he goes from whining to barking you will have to correct him to discourage the behavior. If your dog barks once or twice, ignore him. He might be just saying: *"Excuse me! The door is closed. Will you let me out?"*

If he continues to bark, use the command *"No,"* which will mean to him that this barking is unwanted behavior. If he continues to bark say the word *"No"* again, and tap lightly on the crate. The tapping sound should cause him to stop barking. The noise works because he doesn't understand what the noise is. The noise interrupts his focus on wanting to get out. After he is quiet for a few seconds, tell him he is a good boy again. Remember, you only want to reward the behavior that is acceptable to you.

Should he bark again, say the word "*No*" and lightly tap once on the top. Make sure you are sitting in your chair when you do this. You do not want to be standing in front of the crate. Do not give a lot of attention to the situation. Remain calm and relaxed in your chair and just tap from there. Calmly praise him when he is quiet.

Your tapping should be loud enough that he stops his bark. If you tap too softly, he will continue to bark. Simply adjust your tapping. Make the tap a bit firmer the next time. On the other hand, do not tap too firmly starting out. The tap should not frighten the dog. It is simply meant to redirect.

In the beginning of this training stage, his time in the crate should be less than five minutes. Once he is able to remain quiet for about 30 seconds open the door and invite him out. Tell him he is a good boy with lots of praise, or give him a treat. Be sure you expect him to wait until he is invited out, and don't allow him to rush out of the crate.

Although the dog only spent a few minutes inside the crate, this exercise is very significant. You are creating a positive association with being inside the crate.

For the next few minutes, play with your dog. Don't wait too long to do the exercise again because the first exercise is still fresh in his mind.

If your dog got super excited about the praise and playtime, take some time to calm his energy before you repeat the exercise. Pick up another dog treat, give him the command "*Kennel up,*" and toss the treat to the back. Again, after he goes inside, quietly close the door behind him and sit down in your chair.

Sitting down in your chair may seem kind of silly. It helps to keep the energy level and your intensity low. When he comes to the crate door, tell him: *"Good boy,"* and *"Stay."* Telling him to stay may also seem silly, but we are looking to the future of traveling when you will tell your dog to stay behind in a hotel room or in your RV. You are training your pet to understand that he is supposed to remain where you place him.

At this time in the training, it isn't important that he lay down inside the crate, although that would be preferred. For the first few times, we just need him to be inside the crate without whining or barking. Continue until he can be inside the crate for about 5 or 10 minutes without whining or barking.

Don't peek inside, as you need to have your attention on something other than the dog in the crate. So watch TV, or read, or do whatever, but stay close by and in sight. Do not leave the area this soon in the training. You will get to that later on.

Once you get to a point where you see him relax, stretch the time out a little before you let him out of the crate. Do this exercise not more than three times in your first day. Please do not rush through this stage of the training or push forward too quickly. As we mentioned before, you are creating a positive memory of the experience of being inside the crate.

Although tapping on the crate seems to work best for us, there are other methods that you can use to get the same results. We will cover a few here.

You can use a soda can with pennies or pebbles inside of it. Grab an empty soda can and put some pennies inside of it or some pebbles. Put some tape over the opening of the can so when you shake it, the pebbles or rocks will not fly out. Leave the can on top of the crate. When your dog barks, pick up the can, say *"Fido, no"* and give the can a quick shake. The noise produced will have the same effect as the noise created by tapping.

Here is another distraction: Say the word *"No,"* and then clap your hands loudly one time. You can use other devices or techniques. Different ones may work for your pet. Choose one method and use it consistently.

Be aware of your own energy and state of mind. Are you calm? Is your voice calm or stressed? Even when you do not think the dog can read your level of frustration, know that he can. Dogs read your body language and can pick up on your state of mind. Always train your dog in a calm and nurturing way. You want Fido to see that you are relaxed. You are in your chair relaxing - no big deal. Your dog can lay down in the crate and relax - no big deal. If you stand in front of the crate, he will think he needs to stand up inside because you are going to do something and he wants to do it too.

Continue with this exercise over several days. Extend the time he stays inside until he is so relaxed, he falls asleep. That is about as relaxed as you can get him. Depending on what level of anxiety your pet has, this could take a few days. Once he gets to this level, he will no longer have any fear of the crate. Now the only time he should whine is when he needs to go to the bathroom.

You may wonder how long can the dog stay in the crate? The only limiting factor that you should be concerned with is how long until he needs to go to the bathroom. He will need to go to the bathroom long before he needs food or water. Exercise him properly prior to the crate time.

At this point in your training, your dog should feel quite comfortable spending time inside the crate while you are nearby. If your pet is not totally comfortable while you are sitting down watching TV, do not proceed to the next section. Only move forward with the training when you are both able to relax for at least half an hour.

Stay in the Crate Unsupervised

Now that your dog is comfortable inside his crate, you can work on leaving him inside unsupervised.

He should be at a point now, where he goes into the crate and lays down. Either chewing on a toy, resting or sleeping. Proceed to the next level of crate training only if he has accepted the crate as a safe place where he is comfortable to close his eyes and sleep.

For this next exercise, the crate can remain in the same area next to your comfy chair, as long as you can also go someplace where you are outside of his view. It would be good to have a nearby room, like the kitchen, where you are out of sight, but he can still hear you.

Leave the Room

Place Fido inside the crate and close the door. Start the exercise by sitting down as usual and relax. Wait for Fido to relax for a few minutes. He should lay down on his comfy bed or chew on his toy. Now get up from your chair, look inside the crate and tell him he is a good boy and to *"Stay."* Walk out of sight and carry on a conversation with someone or if needed, with yourself. The idea is to let him know that although he cannot see you, you are still nearby.

Let the conversation be very calm. Please do not talk about Fido, and what a good dog he is. You don't want him to hear his name and think you want him to come to the kitchen with you! You have taken away the visual stimulus at this stage in the training, but he still has the audio stimulus. Even though he cannot see you, he can hear you and knows that you're not too far away. Hearing you will provide some comfort to him in the beginning stages of being left alone in the crate.

When you walk into the kitchen, Fido should remain calm and not whine or bark. If this is the case, continue with your conversation for a few minutes. Then return to your chair, but do not say anything to Fido. Sit down to watch TV or read your book for a little while.

Repeat the process again. The second time you go to the kitchen, remain longer but be sure to talk. You want Fido to hear you and know you are still close by. This time when you return to the crate you will let him come out, praise him and pet him a lot. This is a big success for both of you!

If your Fido whines a little bit when you are out of sight, that's okay. As you did when you sat in the chair and he whined, do not converse with your pet. It only encourages the behavior that you do not want. Stay in the kitchen and see what he does next. He either settles down or starts barking. After he settles down, return to your chair, sit down and tell him he's a good boy and continue to watch TV.

If he barks once, do nothing. Continue with your conversation. If he barks more than three times, say his name, and firmly say the word "No!" from where you are in the other room. By now he should be conditioned to the "No" and stop his barking. Wait a few minutes and return to your chair.

If he continues to bark after you told him "Fido, no," walk back over to the crate, say his name and the word "No," while at the same time tapping on the crate once. If you used another redirect, substitute it for the tapping. Tap only once and return to the other room. If the first tap did not get the desired response, you can come back and tap a little firmer to stop his barking.

Do not carry on a conversation with your pet. You only say "Fido, no" and do the tap. There should be no other conversing. Stay around until he settles down. If need be, sit down in the chair to get him back to a relaxed state. Then go back to the kitchen. Talk, but not to him! He will begin to understand that barking will not result in attention for him.

As with the previous exercise, just relax and take your time. If your dog starts barking and you do not immediately do the correction, it's okay. As he is barking, take a deep breath, think about what you want to do and go do it. It is not the end of the world if your dog is barking in the crate. Don't get frustrated or upset. It is more important that you convey to your pet that you are calm and everything is fine.

If he gets unruly and barks a lot, it means he is not ready for this step. Don't open the crate at this time to let him out. Go back to the previous stage, and sit nearby. Make sure he is totally comfortable and relaxes by lying down and even closing his eyes. Then let him out of the crate.

Leave for Longer Periods of Time

Once your dog is used to the crate and will stay in it for longer while you are at home, you can start leaving him in the crate while you are out and about. We recommend you give him a special chew toy that will keep him busy for a longer period of time. We often use raw soup bones that we purchase at the local grocery store.

If your dog barks a lot when left home alone, it could be because he can hear outside noises. Provide some background noise and drown out any outside noises by leaving your radio or TV on for him. It is best to choose a talk show or calming music.

Start to leave the home for only a few minutes at a time. You can go to the mailbox or just out into the carport. If your dog barks while you are gone, it is a good indication that you need to spend more time on the previous exercise. Once he is comfortable and relaxed in the crate, even when you are out of sight, he will be fine when you leave your home.

Whenever you return, do so in a calm and relaxed state. Do not make a big deal out of coming home. If you give a lot of hyper excited attention to your dog whenever you come home, he will associate the homecoming with hyper excitement.

When you first arrive, pay no attention to him in the crate. Calmly put your things away, then walk up to the crate and let him come out in a very quiet manner. Once he is outside the crate, you can pet him and interact. This will ensure that he associates getting out of the crate with a calm and relaxed manner.

Chapter 5

Potty on Command

To teach your dog to go relieve himself on command may seem trivial, but it is so very helpful when you are traveling. The unusual surroundings and the excitement of travel often distract a dog from doing his thing. As you stop for food and gas, your dog may be too excited to think about going potty. You can see how teaching him to relieve himself on command would be very useful.

Dogs that are not usually walked on a daily basis, often do not want to relieve themselves while on the leash. The exercise in this chapter is a good way to prepare your dog to do his business on-leash.

In Chapter 7 you will read about our trip to Venice Beach and Jaeger's incident on the boardwalk. For now, just take our word for it - you want to train your dog to relieve himself before you take him to any crowded area, like a street market or into a patio restaurant.

Choose a command you want to use. We use: "*do your biz*" for our dogs, but you can use anything that you are comfortable with. Select a second command, such as, *"outside,"* for signaling your dog to go outside for a walk, or if you want to see if he needs to go to the bathroom.

The command you use to signal to go outside needs to be different from the command that will ask the dog to relieve himself.

Pick up the leash and collar after you use the command for "outside." If you pick up the leash and collar before you use the command, he will get excited over the leash and collar, not over the command to go outside. Do not use the command "*do your biz*" inside the home, unless you are training your dog to use a piddle pad inside the house.

"Do Your Biz"

Walk your dog to the area that you want him to relieve himself. Let him sniff around. Use the command "*do your biz*" or whatever command you selected. Do not play with him or walk around a lot. It is best to remain in a certain area, where you want him to relieve himself.

While he is in the process of relieving himself, say the command: "*do your biz*" again. Then praise him: "*Good dog!*"

Do this every time you walk your dog and soon he will associate the command with relieving himself.

As you teach him to go to the bathroom on command, keep your manner calm. Don't get the dog all excited by using an excited voice or body language. Excitement will distract your dog. He will get hyper and you will need to calm him back down to be able to do any training. After he has done at least one of his businesses, praise him and then go for a walk for exercise.

Start using the two new commands every time you take your dog for his walk. Just follow the usual routine of taking him to an area where he does his business and say the command "*do your biz*" when he is relieving himself.

If you are traveling with a small dog or a puppy, consider training your pet to do his biz on a piddle pad. This way, you can let your dog use the bathroom anywhere.

Training your dog to use the pad can be very helpful, especially if you travel a lot by airplane. Although most airports have outdoor dog areas for traveling pets, it can be difficult to find enough time to exit the secure area in-between flights. When your pet is trained to use the piddle pad, you can allow him out of the crate and let him do his business on the pad in a public restroom or another private area. The pad can then be disposed of like a human diaper.

Chapter 6

The Travel Vehicle

This section will help you get your pet ready for long distance driving. Traveling with your pet should be a fun experience for both of you. Most dogs love traveling by automobile and are usually excited to hop in the car to go for a ride. If you have a puppy or a dog that has not been in a vehicle before, start this process well in advance of your trip. Finding out that your pet is nervous in a vehicle or does not behave well in a car when you start your trip is not going to be fun for you or your pet. A misbehaving dog is also very distracting and can be extremely dangerous while you drive. Please be sure to condition your dog properly for travel in any type of vehicle!

Remember your dog wants to be with you and will associate the vehicle with being able to go with you. On the other hand, if being in the car is not comfortable for Fido, it can cause nervousness, whining, inability to lay still, excessive drooling and even car sickness.

You may already take your dog with you on short rides to the dog park or the vet prior to your travel, and you have already established some familiarity with the car. You have taught your dog to lay down in the back seat or the cargo area of your SUV. Please do not let your dog ride in the bed of your pickup truck, unless you have him in a crate and the crate is secured in the bed of the truck.

While riding in the car, your dog should lay down quietly in his spot until you get to where you are going, and should not jump around inside the vehicle while you are driving. He may get up from time to time to look out the window, but for the most part, he should be sitting or laying in his designated spot.

Use the Crate

If your dog is restless in the vehicle and tends to jump around, we highly recommend to have him travel in a crate. It is dangerous to have any dog jumping around, especially if you are the only person in the vehicle. The crate allows you to concentrate on driving, while Fido is secure and stays out of trouble. Refer back to the crate training exercises from Chapter 4 so your dog is comfortable in the crate.

When you use the crate in your vehicle place it so the dog can see you. In the beginning stages of training put the crate in the back seat with the door facing toward you. You want him to be able to see you and you can see him.

Don't forget to secure the crate in the vehicle. You don't want to hit the brakes and have it fly through the car. With small size crates use the seat belt to fasten it to the back seat. Larger crates can be secured with cargo belts or wedged in between things to keep them steady.

Prepare a Place for Your Dog

Before you do anything with Fido, decide where you want your pet to travel in the car. This will largely depend on the dog's size and temperament. Although a small dog can ride in the front seat area, he is NEVER allowed to distract you while you are driving. It is usually best that he travels in the back seat. Larger dogs need to be in the back seat or in the cargo area behind the back seat. Many vehicles allow you to lay down your seats. That can create more room and is another great way to travel with your dog.

If you decide to have the dog in the car without a crate, prepare an area where you want the dog to lay down. Bring a blanket or dog bed and place it in his spot. Make sure there are no items laying around that could shift during the car ride. You don't want anything to hit or fall on your dog and scare him.

Dogs riding in a seat, should be secured with a car harness and buckled in. Special dog seat belts are sold in pet stores and online. Check our website at ModernCanineServices.com under travel accessories to view our product recommendations.

If you do not want to buckle him in and he is small enough, you can get a box and put a dog bed or blanket in it. This way, he is more secure when you go around corners or stop. He won't fall all over and you will not be distracted or want to reach over and grab him.

For larger dogs, you can also get a blanket that is made to hang from the back of the driver seats and covers the floor area, so the dog does not fall off the seat into the floor area.

It is also possible to get a wire or nylon separator. These can be fastened between the back seat and the cargo area. They are made to keep the dog confined to the back of the vehicle. We highly recommend this if you have an SUV or another vehicle with a cargo area.

Once you decide where he will travel in the car make that a regular spot. You can put down a towel or his blanket, or use his crate. Each time you put him in the car he will know that is where he needs to go.

Keep his spot free of clutter and allow enough room for the dog to comfortably lay down. You can stack things around him, but be sure they will not shift or fall on him.

If he is going to travel in his crate, place his blanket or towel and a toy inside. Place it so he can see other passengers or you in the car. This way he can look out of his crate and see his family and know all is well. It will help him not get anxious or car sick.

Although small dogs will usually be able to move around the car, you should have at least one spot that he can go to get away from everyone. It might be on the floor or it might be on the armrest or an empty space on a seat. Wherever you decide that is, you can place a towel or dog bed.

At no time should the dog be allowed to go over to the driver's side of the car. If you think it's cute to have your little dog peek out the window, let the passenger hold him in their lap. It is just not a safe practice to let any dog over on the driver's side of the car. It is up to the driver to enforce that rule. If he comes over on to the driver's side, the driver should ask the passenger to take him away. If you do not have anyone else in the car, use your right arm to push him away from you. Use the command "No" and tell the dog to go to his spot.

Once you have decided where Fido is going to stay in the car, try to make that his regular spot. Don't rearrange the seating unless absolutely necessary.

Car Exercises

In this first exercise, Fido will learn to get in and out of the car and to lay in his spot and be calm. Do this with the vehicle turned off. We recommend you practice loading and unloading the dog several times.

Make sure this is a calm exercise. We so often see people get their dogs all excited about going somewhere in the car. Then they wonder why Fido is jumping around the vehicle and won't settle down. You may be tempted to open the car door and let Fido jump in while you tell him; *"Fido, let's go for a ride"* in a happy excited voice. You may think you are motivating your dog to have a pleasant experience with you. However, it is more beneficial to calmly put on the leash and collar and walk up to the car. Remember, you show your dog how you want him to behave. If you make this an excited, rushing around exercise, you encourage that state of mind and will get it every time you load the dog.

At first, practice getting your dog in and out of the car before you are ready to drive anywhere. Park the car in a secure area and have Fido on the leash. You just want your dog to jump in and out of the car comfortably. For this part of the exercise, you can use toys or treats. If your dog is too small or elderly and cannot get into the vehicle by himself, consider getting a step or a ramp. It is always better for the dog to get in and out of the vehicle by themselves, rather than being lifted and put into the car.

We use a ramp with our pickup truck, as it sits much higher off the ground than our car. The ramp is great for our senior dog, Jaeger, who has arthritis in this front legs and cannot jump out of the truck anymore. It has also proven beneficial for our smaller dog, Heidi, and was instrumental in teaching our puppy, Apollo, to get in and out of the truck.

How to Get in and out

You can throw a ball into the car so he can jump in and retrieve it and bring it back out. You can put a treat on the seat or any other fun way of getting him in the car. You do not want to put your dog into the car. Sometimes you can go sit in the back seat and call your dog to you. And then you climb out of the car and let him follow you. Let him figure out how to get into the car. It might take a few minutes, but he has to figure it out. If he wants to get into the car but he does not know how, help him into the car at first. But make sure you let him figure out how to get in and out of the car on his own four paws.

Now that your dog has figured out how he can get in and out of the car, it is time to teach him to wait for you to invite him to enter and exit. As with other doors, your dog should not rush in or out of the car door. This will ensure his safety as you are traveling. You don't want him to jump out of your vehicle at a busy freeway rest stop. He could get hurt or lost. Practice with the leash and collar on first, so you can control the getting in and out from now on.

Respect the Car Door

Open the car door and make Fido wait to be invited to jump in. If he rushes the door, open the door only slightly and gently close it, if he tries to squeeze through. This is very similar to the door exercise in Chapter 3. Make sure he looks at you and then give him the command to go in.

Do the same as you have the dog exit the vehicle. The most important part is to be consistent with this. Do not sometimes allow him to jump in uninvited and other times require him to wait.

If you are using the crate, leave both the car door and the crate door open to load the dog. Put the leash and collar on your pet and walk to the car. Encourage the dog to get into the car and use your command for him to get into the crate. After he goes in, quietly close the door and tell him he is a good boy. You do not want to sit there and talk to him in front of the crate. Just close the door and get into the driver seat.

If your dog will travel without the crate, load him quietly. When the dog is in the car, you can use praise, but don't get him too excited.

Inside the Car

Load the dog into the car and wait for him to settle in. Don't rush this part. If you just make him sit or lay on command, but he is ready to jump up, that is not settled in. You are looking for him to relax in the car. Sit in the seat up front and give him time to settle. It is best to ignore him until he decides to sit or lay down. Once he is settled you can praise him. Only reward and encourage the behavior you want. When you give him attention when he is still excited, you are encouraging that behavior.

Once he is calm, ask him to exit the vehicle in a calm fashion. Remember he will enter and exit the vehicle in unfamiliar and busy places, so make sure that you are in control of him at all times. He should not jump out of the car just because you opened the door. You will expect him to wait until you invite him out. Practice loading him in and out of the car and have him settle into his spot several times.

Now it is time to take him for short rides. At first, make sure you are only training and don't try to run your errand at the same time. Your mind will be your errand and not on training your dog. As with all training, it is important to be calm and patient. The car ride needs to be a good experience so that Fido can build confidence. If you train while you are distracted or in a rush, you risk making the car ride a bad memory. This can make the dog reluctant to get into the vehicle in the future.

It is helpful to drive with a second person in the vehicle. This way one person can supervise and control the dog, while the other drives.

No matter how small your dog is, dogs are NEVER allowed in your lap while you are driving, ever! We see people with little dogs standing on their laps looking out the window. Although very cute, it is just not a safe way to drive your car. Please do not get in the habit of letting your dog on your lap when you are the driver.

For larger dogs, have the passenger sit near where the dog is and hold on to the leash. The leash is to ensure that the dog does not jump around the vehicle and distract the driver. We do not recommend that you tie the leash in the vehicle, as the dog can get wrapped up in it. If you want to secure the dog in the vehicle, use a crate or a car safety harness with seat belt buckle.

Decide where you are going to drive to. Make it a short drive, less than 15 minutes. More important than the drive is where you are going. Make sure it is a fun place, like a dog park or a nearby park. Choose a place your dog will enjoy.

If you are the one driving the car, do not participate in the training process. Let the other person take care of the dog.

During the ride, have the person simply hold the leash. If the dog is quiet and lays down or sits nicely and looks outside, it is OK to pet him. However, if he is whining and uncomfortable, do not pet him and do not try to console him. Petting him is telling him his behavior is acceptable and you are sending the wrong message. Just ignore his behavior and remain calm. You can have a calm conversation with the other person. This will help to calm the dog. When you get to your destination, play with your dog or take him for a wonderful walk.

The return trip will offer another training opportunity. You can switch roles and have the other person drive or you can drive again. If you normally will be doing all the driving, then get the dog accustomed to you being in the driver seat and unavailable to him.

Extend the amount of time you drive and make sure there is always some fun walk or playtime at the end of your trip together. Most dogs quickly settle into the car. If your dog remains restless and overly scared, or overly excited while you drive, it is best to go to using the crate for your car travel.

Wait to talk to your dog until after you turn off your car. Keep the excitement low until you have taken the dog out of the crate and out of the car. If you talk excitedly, the dog will get hyper and you will have a hard time getting the crate door open and the leash on the dog. He will get rowdy and jump out of the car. The process of getting in and out of the car needs to be calm. Quietly open the door to the crate and put the leash on the dog's collar, so you have control over him. Calmly invite him to come out of the crate and the car. Now you can pet him and praise him a lot!

Go and have fun with your dog. Repeat the process when returning home. Repeat the exercise a few times and extend the travel time. Your goal in this exercise is to have your pet lay down quietly in the crate or in his spot while you are driving and to be able to have him enter and exit the car calmly and without hesitation.

Get Your Dog used to Travel in Your RV

As with any training, it is best to start with short trips in the RV, before you go on a vacation or long drive. Although the RV has many advantages, it has a very different feel to your dog. For one, there are going to be a lot of noises, as the things in the storage cabinets and the furniture moves around during travel. Make sure you take the time to slowly get your dog accustomed to this. It can be a frightening experience, if not done correctly. You want to make sure that your dog is comfortable in the RV before you start your trip.

Start by letting your dog go in and out of the camper so that he can get used to the smells and surroundings.

If your RV is in a storage area, take your dog there so that he can go in and out of it a few times before you get on the road. If your RV attaches to your vehicle and you tow it, you will only need to take your dog in and out a few times since he will not be in the camper during travel time. If you travel in a motorhome, you will want to take a couple of short road trips with your dog before you go on the long trip.

We will cover how to set up your RV before you go out on your trip. If you are fortunate enough to be able to have your RV in your yard, this will make the exercise much easier. But either way, you want to let your dog go in and out of the camper a few times before the road trip. As with the car, it is best to let the dog enter and exit on his own four paws. We have included exercises to teach the dog to manage the RV stairs and to get set up in the vehicle in the following sections.

Prepare the Interior of the Camper for Your Dog

Similar to your car, your RV will need a spot just for your dog. Whether you are driving down the road in a motorhome or are camping with a bumper pull, your dog will need his own spot that he can go to and feel comfortable. Think about how you set up your personal space to make it comfortable for you.

When you decide on where to put your dog, ponder a couple of things first. Will he be in the way when he is laying down? Most of the time you will want your dog to go somewhere and lay down out of the way. This is not always easy, as RVs can be rather small and the walkways are often narrow.

A smaller dog can easily find a spot, but if you have a medium to large dog, you will need to consider where the dog and his dog bed or crate can be placed without being in the way.

In our Fifth Wheel, we actually took out one of the reclining chairs to create room for a big dog bed right near the door. This allows our 95 pound Chesapeake Bay Retriever, Jaeger, to have a comfortable spot in the living area, but not right in the walkway. Jaeger loves his bed. He can see out the open door when we are in a campsite and at the same time he can see everything that goes on inside. All without being in the way and getting stepped on.

Taking out furniture to make room for your dog may not be an option for you. Many of our friends allow the dog to be on the bed or dinette area during travel to keep the dog from having to be in the narrow walkway.

If your dog has to get up to get out of your way every time you go to the refrigerator, it may not be a great place. If you let him have a spot on the couch or dinette area while traveling, consider that he will also want to be in it when you are camped someplace overnight. Can it still be his spot?

Not everyone will have a 30-foot RV with lot's of options. Try to put a little thought into where you would like your dog to be able to sleep and be out of the way. Larger dogs will need more room, but even a tiny dog needs his special place that he can call his own. He might have a spot that he likes to go when you are in the camper, but he might want his own bed when no one is home with him.

Once you have selected his spot, put his blanket or dog bed there. Use a dog bed that he has already used, rather than a brand new one. Dogs feel more comfortable with surroundings that smell familiar. So if you use his dog bed, you put that familiarity into the motorhome or camper for him. If you are going to use his crate in the camper, just place his comfortable bed inside.

Next, you will want to have a storage area where you keep his treats and toys. We use big rawhide bones, Kongs, tennis balls, and other smelly treats that our dogs love. When they first come into our Fifth Wheel, they immediately go to the box and look for their toys. Finding their familiar items in the camper every time puts them at ease and makes them feel comfortable and secure.

Decide on where you will water and feed the dog. More than likely, you will not have the water and food out while you are driving. This is for the times when the RV is parked for lunch or overnight.

We prefer to water our dogs outside whenever possible, mainly because we have our Chessy, Jaeger, who is a sloppy drinker and likes to splash water all over the place. We have a water bowl under the sink. We place it just outside the RV door when we are parked. While camping, we spend most of our time outside the RV. Jaeger can splash water all over, without making a mess inside. This works well in most situations. There have been a few times when the weather was such that this set-up did not work, and we brought the water bowl inside and placed a good size towel under it.

The main intent here is to make the camper his home and a comfortable place to be. Spend some time thinking about where your dog will have a spot and how you will water and feed him.

First Impressions: Start Out on the Right Paw

Before you take your dog into your camper, set it up for him. We know you've heard the paraphrase "There is no second chance for a good first impression". This is a good phrase to keep in mind when introducing a dog to a new area. This section is written for a timid dog or the dog that does not like change or uncertainty. If you have a dog that runs in and checks out the whole place, you are already ahead of the game.

Open some blinds and windows. Place a couple of dog treats around the inside of the RV. Also place some treats onto the steps of the camper. Set out his bowl of water and food where you plan to feed him while camping.

Now that the camper is ready, bring Fido on the leash and walk him up to it. Keep your energy calm. As you walk up to the camper, be aware of your dog's body language. Is his tail in a happy position? Is his head up and curious about what you are going to explore with him? Or is he timid and cautious?

If you walk your dog up to the camper for the first time and he is concerned about it, walk around the outside first. Let him smell the tires, the bumper, and all the exterior things. Walk back to the front door. Make sure that the door is open when you come around.

You prepared the treats on the steps of the camper. Let him eat the treats on the first step and see if he will go towards the next step. Do not pull him up the steps, if he can physically make it. It is best if he enters by himself on his own four paws. Resist the urge to lift him into the RV. If he eats the treat on the first step, but will not climb up the second step, you can sit inside the camper and let him be at the steps. Give him time to figure out how to go up the steps.

Walking up RV steps, to a dog, can be a scary situation in and of itself. When a dog walks up to RV retractable steps, they can see through the steps out the back. This scares a lot of dogs.

It is very important that you do not pull him to you or drag him up the steps. Remember, you might be teaching him to climb the steps at the same time as you introduce him to the camper, so take your time. Once he puts his rear feet onto the first level of the stairs, you are home free. The motivating factor for him to come into the camper is you and the treats.

On a side note, it is possible that the RV steps are too steep for an older dog. Of course, you would already know your dog's capabilities in regards to steps. There are foldable and retractable ramps that you can purchase at a pet store or you can build your own.

RV Steps Exercise

Sit at the top of the stairs, inside the RV and coax him into coming to you. Do not pull him to you. It must be on his terms as to how he is going to get to you. Offer him a treat and lots of verbal praise for coming to you.

If he is very reluctant to go up the stairs of your camper, take a towel and but it onto the steps, forming it to fit. This will provide a backing and can relieve the dog's fear of the openness of the steps.

Continue the exercise until he easily enters and gets out of the camper. Once he is comfortable going in and out of the RV you are ready to move on to the next step.

Introduce Fido to the Camper

Take him into the camper and right to his spot. Let him sniff his dog bed and take out a treat from his toy box or from the cabinet in which you keep his treats. If he eats the treat and is relaxed that is very good. Once inside the camper, you can take the leash off and let him find all the other treats. Keep the energy low and calm. You don't want him to be in a hyper excited state inside the small place. Teach him right away to be calm inside the camper. If he is timid and not exploring, you can encourage him by walking around with him.

Remember, this is not "his" camper yet, so keep an eye on him to make sure he does not mark any areas. If he is wandering around the camper, checking out the place, that is good. You can start to make yourself at home also. You could turn on the generator and start the AC, or turn on the heater and make noises that he is likely to encounter while you are camping. Let him get used to the sounds and vibrations of the camper. The camper will shift and there are noises associated with your moving around. Don't just sit down in a chair. Walk around, open cabinet doors, and do some of the stuff that you might do while camping.

When you start a new sound and you notice that he is very concerned about it, don't pet him in an anxious state. Rather redirect his attention by offering a smell, like a favorite treat. Do not feed him the treat, rather redirect his attention by holding the treat in the closed hand, and waving it in front of his nose. Just move the hand back and forth slowly. The scent will redirect his focus away from what might have scared him. He will learn to associate the camper with the pleasant smell of the treat.

If he is relaxed and wants to walk around, allow him to check out the camper. After a while, he will lay down on his own. He may not lay down on his bed but may pick a spot that is near you on the floor, this is fine. Once he lays down, you can praise him and pet him.

On the Road with the Motorhome

Now that your dog is comfortable going in and out of the camper you want to teach him how to be comfortable inside the vehicle, as it moves down the road. This is for motorhomes only. If you travel with your camper in-tow, your dog must travel in the tow vehicle with you.

As with car travel, it would be best to have another person with you on the first few trips. Leave the leash on him for the first short trips to see how he reacts. Most dogs like traveling in the RV and will quickly get comfortable with this mode of travel. But traveling in a motorhome comes with all kinds of noises. Things vibrate and shift during the driving process.

Never pet or praise your dog if he is stressed, whines or paces around. Only give attention and praise when he is calm. When Fido pants anxiously and whines, just ignore him. Since he is leashed, it should be easy for the passenger to keep him out of trouble.

Never allow a dog to get overly excited while in the RV. It can be dangerous to have any size dog jump around and distract your driving. To contain him, one good idea is to use a dog car seat belt harness to secure him in the dinette area. Another idea is to consider using his crate, if your dog shows signs of anxiety, like drooling or panting. The crate will offer him an added sense of security, as long as he has learned to be crated properly.

Chapter 7

Unfamiliar Places

Now that your dog has learned to walk properly on the leash, respects open doors, and is comfortable inside your car or the recreational vehicle, you can start to introduce him to different places and situations.

Once you are on the road, you will need to take your dog almost everywhere you go. It's hard to prepare for all the different scenarios, but you can prepare your dog by taking him to busy places, such as Farmer's Markets or outdoor festivities.

When we first started traveling with our dogs, we took Jaeger to the beach in California. As a Chesapeake Bay Retriever, he right away fell in love with the Ocean. California has some pretty awesome dog beaches. Jaeger could be off leash and swim and chase the waves all day. In the evening, we took the dog with us to Venice Beach, a popular and very busy area north of Los Angeles. The area was buzzing with tourists, street musicians and merchants. Jaeger was fine until a few young people came down the boardwalk on their skateboards. He did not like the sound of the skateboards coming up behind him. In his fear, he backed out of his collar and he got so nervous, he ended up with diarrhea (right in the middle of the boardwalk).

Three things we learned that day:
1. Make sure you expose your dog ahead of time to a lot of different noisy and busy places, so he learns to be calm and relaxed when you are out having fun on your vacation.
2. Use your training collar to secure your dog in unfamiliar places.
3. ALWAYS walk your dog and have him do his business, BEFORE you go to an area that has a lot of people.

For additional security, you can use his training collar in addition to his regular collar and attach his leash to both. The training collar won't fall off the dog and he cannot back out of it. It is a good way to ensure you won't lose your dog.

In case you are wondering, Jaeger was fine. He seeks his security from being close to us, so even without the leash and collar, he never moved away from us. Still, it was an uncomfortable situation.

You should practice with your dog in busy downtown areas. Walk him up and down different types of stairways and narrow walkways. Get him used to crowded areas. It's not just about different noises and smells that your dog will need to get used to, but also different types of surfaces he may need to walk on.

When we took our dogs to Seattle, Washington, we wanted to see the Ballard locks. It is a popular tourist attraction and there were a lot of people visiting that day. When we got to the main area, where the boats were being raised and lowered, Birgit noticed the walkway that lead over the water to the lock was a metal see-through grid. Birgit's first reaction was to tell Jim to go ahead and see the lock up close, while she would wait with the two dogs at a nearby bench. Jim, being a dog trainer, thought it was a great opportunity to see if the dogs would be comfortable. He encouraged Birgit to walk Jaeger onto the metal gangway. Jaeger actually never hesitated. He just walked right out to the lock area and stood by Birgit's side while she watched the boats come into the lock. Heidi, the smaller dog, was tucked under Jim's arm since her tiny paws could have easily slipped through the coarse metal grid surface.

You never know what type of walking surface you may encounter on a vacation trip. We've taken our dogs over bridges with wooden planks that were swinging high above a gorge. They have been on paddle boards, narrow steep hiking trails, in elevators, and on moving sidewalks.

You may not plan to do a lot of adventurous stuff, but there are a lot of unexpected situations waiting for you and your dog. We believe one of the most important travel preparations is to make sure your dog is comfortable in unfamiliar places and feels safe wherever you take him because he has learned to trust you.

Here are a few exercises you can do with your dog prior to taking him on vacation. The following training exercises expose your dog to some unfamiliar places and in the process teach him to rely on you for guidance and safety.

Hometown Adventure Exercises

1. Get your dog used to being out in public places

Practice by taking your dog with you to a few busy places around your home town. Make it a regular habit to take your dog to the Farmer's Market or an outdoor event. This will teach him to be around a lot of other people, noises and smells. Make sure he is comfortable walking through crowded areas and is well-behaved. He should be walking calmly by your side and not bark or lunge at the leash when he sees other dogs or distractions.

2. Practice walking on different types of surfaces and through obstacles and distractions.

Expose your dog to as many different surfaces and distractions as possible. Find a local skateboard park and take your dog near it. The sounds and fast moving skateboards are hard to get used to for many dogs. Being accustomed to these noises will help as you are out in unusual surroundings. Find bridges in local parks that may have wooden planks with sections you can see through, as this is another tough one for dogs. Go up and down different types of stairways and take your dog into an elevator.

3. Take your dog to local restaurants

Have you taken your dog out for dinner? Can you eat and enjoy your meal with him under the table, or is he getting himself wrapped up in his leash and is restless? Practice until he is calm and lays down under the table, out of everyone's way. Don't allow your dog to sit on the chair or sniff around the tabletops! Other patrons will not like the idea of your dog having licked the plates or the tabletops.

4. Teach him to be left by himself in unfamiliar surroundings

This may be the hardest lesson to teach. Find an area that you can leave your dog by himself and see how he reacts. Most dogs will whine or bark when left by themselves in unfamiliar surroundings.

You can start the exercise by leaving your dog with another person, while you walk out of sight. If you are by yourself, tie the dog up to a tree, put him in a "sit" or "stay" and walk out of sight. It is a good idea to have a familiar item for him to lay on, so bring your dog's bed or blanket. Only leave for a few minutes and then come back.

Your dog should remain calm and wait for your return. If he whines or barks while you are out of sight, resist making a big deal out of your return. Act matter of fact, take the leash and walk a few steps, then repeat the exercise. Practice a few times. Slowly extending the amount of time you are out of sight, until you can leave your dog by himself for about 5 minutes.

Taking Fido with you on short day trips will teach him to be well-behaved in all kinds of different situations.

We would love to hear about your experience with unusual places and how your dog managed them. Please come join us in our Facebook group *"Keep Your Paws on the Road"* and share your pictures and stories with our growing community of dog-loving travelers. You can find a link to the Facebook group on our website homepage at ModernCanineServices.com.

Chapter 8

Departure Checklist

Health Certificate and Vaccinations

While you travel with your dog, he will likely be in areas where other dogs and other animals have been. He will be in contact with other dogs, most of them healthy while some may not. You want to make absolutely sure that your dog is healthy, long before you plan to go on your trip. Make an appointment with your veterinarian and discuss your travel plans. Your vet can recommend all the vaccines and shots your pet will need. He can also help you with certificates and papers you may need to travel into foreign countries.

One of the vaccines that your pet will need is a rabies shot. After your dog is given this vaccine, your vet may have to send in the paperwork to your governmental agency, depending on your city's animal control laws. Start the vaccine process early, and give yourself enough time to deal with the paperwork, so you have all your dog's vaccines up to date and enough time for the paperwork to be submitted and returned to you before you start traveling.

When you finally get those documents and vaccine records, you will be tempted to put them in a folder at your house. Remember to make copies and pack them with your other important documents that you travel with. Even if you don't plan to leave your dog while on the road, there is a good chance that somewhere along your trip you will want to go to an entertainment that won't allow pets. There is always a possibility that you need to find a boarding facility or that you have some kind of emergency, so do not leave without your pet's health records! We recommend you place the paperwork in a zip lock bag, together with a recent photograph of your dog. The picture can be a useful item if your dog gets lost during your travel, away from home.

If you travel outside of the United States, your pet may need a Health Certificate or Pet Passport; in some areas, your dog may be quarantined for a period of time. It is best to research all the rules and check with your veterinarian. We cannot urge you enough to make sure you start the process early so you are ready to travel with your pet's vaccines and documentation in order.

The internet is a great resource to get all the most up to date information on rules and regulations each country has in regards to bringing in live animals. The best source for this information is the country's embassy website. We suggest you do not rely on third party information.

Identifications

Ensure your dog has an identification tag on his collar that has your cell phone number on it. We see a lot of people travel with their dogs, and although the dog has a tag on his collar, it bears the owner's home telephone number. This is something few people consider. Away from home, in another state or even another country, you don't want people to call your home when they find your Fido. You will want them to be able to call right to your cell phone. Make sure you check the information on your dog's tag and be sure it includes your mobile number.

We highly recommend that you have Fido micro-chipped. This is a wonderful way to ensure your dog can be identified in case he is lost. One of the reasons dogs get lost away from home is that their collar breaks. You can see where the ID tag may not be as helpful as you thought. Having Fido chipped means he cannot lose his ID. He can also be identified when he is stolen and someone takes him to a vet. All vets automatically scan for a chip. We know of a person that was able to get their dog back after it was stolen from them. The thief took the dog in for his shots and the vet found out the dog was reported missing. There are a lot of great stories about dogs finding their way home due to the microchip. If your dog isn't micro-chipped, consider getting it done before you travel with him.

If you like a more high-tech, on demand solution, you can look into getting a GPS tracker for your dog's collar. These are small devices, that send a signal you track with your mobile phone, or laptop. They require a monthly subscription and are still rather costly, but they do allow you to find your dog quickly, should he get lost.

Pack with Care

If your dog is on regular medications or supplements, make sure you have enough of them with you to last throughout the trip. You may not be able to find the same brand in another town, so pack the right amount.

For longer trips, you will want to be sure to research your dog food brand and make sure it is available for purchase throughout your travel.

Having your dog food brand available may seem like a sure thing, but if you travel into another state, your local brand of dog food may not be sold. Especially if you plan to travel for a long period of time, or if you plan to go outside the US, we urge you to do some research on your dog food brand.

We recently heard from one of our customers who was traveling to Canada. He had to surrender all his dog food at the border crossing. Surely premium dog food is sold in Canada, but if you have a dog on a special diet for allergies or intolerance, it may cause some unwanted discomforts. We have traveled with pets that had digestive problems and can tell you it does not add value to the vacation experience! We provide more in-depth information on travel diet in Chapter 12.

We have found that having the dog food in a plastic container with a tight fitting lid on it works best. This is much better than to bring the dog food in the bag, as it easily spills over, or can get wet. Get another plastic container for the rest of his stuff. Plan to bring some treats and some of his favorite toys. Bringing familiar items with you will help Fido feel comfortable on the trip. Sometimes people think they want to get all new things for a trip and buy new bedding and dog toys. This is fun for you, but your dog would prefer his old bed and worn toys. These familiar items allow you to bring some of his home with you.

Bring Spare Parts

Pack a second collar and leash. We have been on trips where one of our dog's collar broke and we needed a replacement but were not near any store that carried such items. On one road trip in California, Jim accidentally left both of our dog leashes on the side of the road. Jim remembered them about 10 minutes into driving down the freeway. We ended up turning around to retrieve them - luckily, they were still right where Jim had hung them on a fence. You can see the benefit of having an extra leash with you, can't you?

Everyday Supplies

You want to have the leash and plenty of dog bags readily accessible for when you stop for a rest stop. Have his water bowl and a gallon jug of water in the travel vehicle. Don't rely on having water available wherever you stop. It is best to have some water in the car, so you don't have to go looking for water for your dog. There are great collapsible water bowls that you can bring with you in your backpack or purse when you are on a hiking trail or walking in the city. These have been invaluable to us on our travels.

Plan Ahead for Dog-friendly Alternatives

Consider what type of activities you plan to do while you are traveling and research prior to your trip to see if these activities are dog-friendly. If you are going to visit some tourist attractions, you may not be able to bring Fido along. You will need to figure out what you will do with him.

Some big amusement park or tourist activities will have a boarding kennel that you may wish to keep your pet in. Always call before you show up at the facility to make sure that they offer boarding and that it will be available at the time you travel. Finding out when you arrive that they are full, doing a remodel or permanently closed, is surely going to ruin the day.

We have included a lot of information regarding leaving your dog with someone in Chapter 13. If the tourist attraction does not offer boarding, you need to find a dog daycare, but either way, you will need those current vaccine records.

Pet First Aid Kit

When you travel with your dog, your dog may step into a cactus or get stung by a bee. Here are some useful items we recommend you bring with you as a simple travel first aid kit.

- Diphenhydramine (Benadryl®),
- Hydrogen peroxide
- Tweezers
- Eye dropper or large syringe without needle
- Vet wrap
- Natural eye drops

In the event your dog gets hurt while you are on the road, these items can help. Hopefully, you are in a place where you can get the help of a veterinarian and your pet will be in quick recovery.

Diphenhydramine is an antihistamine that is safe to administer to dogs in case they have an allergic reaction; for example, if your dog is bitten by a spider or stung by a bee. Be sure to check with your vet to get recommendations about proper dosage for your dog.

Hydrogen peroxide can be used to clean out a wound or cut, and can also induce vomiting when your dog has ingested a poisonous item. Again, please be sure to seek the advice of a veterinarian to ensure proper usage.

You can use the eye dropper or large syringe to flush out wounds and natural eye drops are safe to use on most dogs.

In case your dog has gotten into some cacti, make sure you have some tweezers or a tool to remove thorns or spines. A regular hair comb is recommended when you have a dog that got into cholla cactus to remove the larger pieces. You will need the tweezers to remove the spines.

Vet wrap is a non-stick bandage that sticks to itself, but not to your dog's fur. It is very helpful in situations where you want to quickly wrap up a wound or even to use as a gentle muzzle for your dog, if needed.

You should always seek the professional advice of a veterinarian if your dog has been injured.

You might also consider taking a course in pet first aid if you travel frequently with your dogs. We have found the information invaluable.

Pet Insurance

It may be a good idea to research getting a policy for your pet with a Pet Insurance Company. There are several companies that offer coverage for pet health care. Please be sure to read the terms carefully and ask questions about coverage.

If you already have a policy for you dog, you may wish to review the details for your policy, to ensure you are still covered in the area you plan to travel to, as many pet insurance policies have restrictions on where or what they cover.

Part 2

On the Road

Chapter 9

Dog-Friendly Travel

Advanced planning is needed when you travel with your dog in a car. When you travel with people, you can communicate and find out what they need. With a dog, you are 100% in charge of his comfort, well-being, and safety. In addition, there are a lot of places you cannot take your dog, so plan your road trip from a dog-friendly perspective.

Find Dog-friendly Rest Stops

It is okay to stop for your dog only when the humans need to stop. But when you are ready to stop you will need to make sure you find a place nice enough to walk Fido. One person should be responsible during the stop for the dog. Someone else should worry about the fuel and food. If you travel by yourself, make sure you see to Fido first, before you get gas or eat.

Take the dog for a walk in a vacant field or grassy area. Please take notice of the kind of surface your dog will be walking on. We know this might seem a little insignificant. You wear shoes and your dog does not. Especially in extreme heat or cold, it is important to check. Check the surface, by placing your hand palm down on the ground. If you are unable to keep your hand on the ground for some time, your dog will not be able to keep his paws on there either.

It is best to find grassy areas to walk your dog, but that may not always be a valid option. There are canine boots you can purchase in pet stores or online that can protect your dog's feet during hot summer months, or extremely cold conditions. You can also go to our website at ModernCanineServices.com to see our favorite products.

Always keep your dog on the leash when you walk him at any rest stop. You may be tempted to let your dog run free, so he can do his business and get exercise, however, he can easily get hurt or lost if he chases after a rabbit or gets frightened by an unfamiliar noise. Unless you have found a fenced in area in which your dog can safely run free, keep him on the leash at all times.

You need to carry dog bags for cleanup with you at all times while you travel. Please don't rely on finding them available at dog walking areas. It is nice to find such areas, but come prepared to clean up after your dog.

If you travel for long periods of time, don't just stop to let your dog relieve himself, plan to take him for a walk around a park, or open area, so he can get some physical exercise.

Give your dog some water. Offer the water for about 10 minutes. Don't get worried if he does not drink. He may be too excited about the travel. On the other hand, watch that he does not overindulge himself. Some dogs are overexcited and drink a ton of water. Do not give him several refills, as he will likely throw up the water in the car, or he will need to relieve himself within about 20 minutes.

We don't recommend food while you are driving during the day. Wait to feed him when you are ready to stop for the night.

Mealtime

When you travel with your dog, you may be unable to go into a restaurant and eat. Depending on the season, it might be too warm or too cold to leave Fido by himself in the car for long periods of time. It is therefore important that you plan ahead and think about how you want to go about your mealtimes. If the weather permits, you can search for dog-friendly restaurants along your travel route. Not all restaurants advertise that they are dog-friendly, so search for patio restaurants and call ahead to ask if you can bring Fido.

Another option is to go through a drive-thru restaurant or order for carry-out. Find a local park or shady area to eat your meal. Make it a picnic. This way you are relaxed and Fido can be outside for a while before it's back on the road.

Taking Fido to the Restaurant

It has been our experience that many patio restaurants will allow dogs. If possible, call ahead to find out if you can bring Fido. Restaurants have to meet certain guidelines in order to be able to allow pets on their patios. Dogs are never allowed inside a restaurant, so the restaurant will have a separate entrance to the patio area.

When you find a dog-friendly restaurant, make sure your Fido behaves in a way that does not interfere with the dining experience of other guests. Select a table where your dog can lay down and be out of the general area and not within the walking path of waiters or other guests. Do not allow your dog onto the chairs or tables of the restaurant, even if he is small! Consider that there are other guests, some of which may not be as dog-loving as you are. Even if your dog sits in your lap at home, do not allow him to be near the tabletops, plates or silverware at a restaurant. For small dogs, we recommend you bring a dog bed or blanket. Place it on the ground under the table and ask your dog to lay down in it.

Larger dogs are usually comfortable just laying under the table. Your pet should be calm and quiet. He should not bark or whine, even when other dogs are in the area.

You can first practice with your dog in more public areas, such as outdoor food courts or outdoor malls. Get your dog used to being around other people, food, and other dogs and teach him to be quiet and calm.

You might be tempted to leave your dog in the car while everyone goes inside to eat at a nice restaurant. We cannot emphasize enough the dangers of doing this if it is warm or cold. Even though the summer temperature outside the car may seem tolerable, the temperature inside the car will be significantly higher. If you think about this, you know this, because everyone has gotten into a car that was parked in the summer and felt the extreme heat inside the vehicle. It takes only a few moments to heat up inside the car. We cannot stress this enough. NEVER leave your dog in the car by himself for long periods of time. Your dog can suffocate from heat exhaustion within 20 minutes or less. The dilemma with leaving the dog in the car is that there is no air flow. The sun comes through the glass and heats up the air. Even when you leave the windows down the inside of the car will still get too hot, too quickly. Take this warning to heart and don't leave Fido in the car by himself in the summer time!

When you need to go into a store for some reason and you are unable to take the dog with you, one person can stay in the car with the dog. For quick stops, it is possible to leave Fido if it is not in summer weather conditions. Always find a shady spot in which to park the car if it is at all sunny outside. Leave the windows cracked a bit to allow some airflow and make sure you are only going to be gone for a few minutes!

For those of you traveling alone with your dog, here is another option: Jim would leave the engine running with the AC on. He put the emergency brake on and locked the vehicle with a second key. Jim did not have to worry about someone stealing his car as his dogs were protecting it. But use caution if you decide to use this method, as many modern cars will not allow you to lock the doors with the keys still in the vehicle.

Chapter 10

Daily Exercise

During your daily travel time, walk your dog not just for potty breaks, but also for exercise. During longer travel times, it may get boring and you or the passengers may want to play with your dog. Most interaction with the dog inside the car should remain calm and quiet. Certainly, there should never be any roughhousing or tug-of-war. It is best to leave the playtime for rest stops when the dog is outside the vehicle.

Nothing helps a dog feel more relaxed than getting plenty of physical exercise. It is easy to forget to give your dog long vigorous walks when traveling. As humans, we want to just get in the car and go and get to where we need to be. If you make sure that Fido has plenty of opportunities to get rid of his energy, he will be a wonderful travel companion. But if you make him stay in the car and hotel room without much exercise, he can easily turn into a nuisance and start displaying destructive behavior or become overly excited.

Not every town or neighborhood has fenced in dog parks, so there may not be any opportunity to let Fido off leash to run and play. Vigorous walks, meaning, walking not for potty breaks, but walking for exercise, can be just as fun and beneficial as off leash play.

Looking for opportunities to exercise our dogs has been one of the most rewarding tasks in our own travel experience. Very often, while looking for a place to just park and walk for a little while, we have found the most wonderful nature adventures. When we learned to look for exercise opportunities for our dogs, we end up seeing a lot of the areas that we would otherwise pass through. It has taught us to break up our driving time and get out and enjoy the journey.

It is important that you walk your dog, and not have your dog walk you. Don't be tempted to let him sniff and lead you all over the place. Walking for exercise should mean that you walk at a brisk pace with Fido on a loose leash next to you. Thirty minutes, twice a day, should provide a good foundation while you are on the road. You will also feel much better yourself when you make such walks a routine of your travel experience.

Off-leash Opportunities

While walking your dog for 30 to 45 minutes, twice a day, is optimal, it is rewarding to find off-leash opportunities to let your dog roam free and enjoy himself. Whenever you let your dog off leash, you want to be sure you are in a secure environment and you have total control.

The underlying goal in our dog training and behavior modification is always geared towards one thing, and that is voice control of your dog. Wouldn't it be wonderful if your dog were in your car and you opened up your car door knowing that when he jumped out you would have total control, and that he would not take off and run away? Or that you could go on a hike or walk on an off-leash beach and be certain you can call Fido back to you at any time?

We want you to believe that you can control your pet through only your voice, with no leash required. Although most places outside of your home will require Fido to be on a leash, those other places that do not require a leash will be much more enjoyable to both your pet and you when he can wander and smell, and you don't have to worry about him at all.

In Part 1 of this book, you read over essential training for your pet. If you and Fido have gone through the exercises described, he is now responding to you and trusts that you are in control.

In this section, we will introduce you to two new exercises to teach your dog to come back to you when called. You will first practice with him on leash, to properly teach the recall command, and then you can practice the recall in a secure environment, such as a fenced in dog park, to make sure you condition your dog to come to you even if there are distractions. Once your dog has learned the command and you have conditioned him with repeated sessions to respond to the recall without fail, you can take him to other off-leash areas. If he is conditioned to follow your lead, you can take advantage of the many off-leash opportunities that are available in many cities.

Here are a few examples of off-leash opportunities:

- Dog parks
- Dog beaches
- Hikes
- Kayak/Paddle board
- bicycle or horseback rides

The Recall

First, you will teach your dog the command for coming to you. You can do this exercise indoors or outdoors. Please start your training with your dog on the 6-foot leash and use your training collar. Many people try to teach the recall with the dog off-leash, and it can confuse the dog, so you want to start out training this command on leash first.

Decide on your recall command. We use the word "*Come*," but you can use anything you want. When you call your dog to you, use his name first and then the recall command. Most situations that require a recall will have the dog at a distance, distracted by smells or activities. When you call out the dog's name, he will stop and look to you for instructions.

Use treats during your training with the first exercise and give a small treat in addition to praise. However, you can also teach the command without treats.

We personally rarely use treats for teaching the recall, because it is a very important command for the dog to follow and we want to be sure he will come to us, even when he is not receiving a treat. A solid recall can be a lifesaver for your dog, especially when you travel away from home to unfamiliar places.

Teach the Recall

With your dog securely on-leash, walk a few steps with a loose leash and then stop. Let Fido become interested in the surroundings or back away from him a little if he is right next to you.

In the very first stages, we recommend you crouch down and call Fido to you. Say his name and use your verbal command and then reel your dog toward you gently with the leash. When he is right in front of you, praise him and tell him he is a good dog. Repeat this several times, until you no longer need to use the leash to bring him toward you, and he comes to you without you pulling on the leash.

Now, stand up, walk a few steps and this time call him to you without crouching down to his level. You can use your hands to pat your leg to encourage him further. If he doesn't come over after you said his name and gave the command, slightly tug on the leash and bring him to you. Once he is by your side, praise him by petting him and telling him he is a good dog. Repeat this step until he comes without hesitation.

Practice the recall on-leash often and in more public settings while on the walk. This will add some distractions for the dog and you can make sure he learns to follow the command even when he is distracted. Remember that training takes teaching and conditioning to form a lasting behavior. Do not proceed until the dog will respond to your recall on-leash without hesitation. If you want to, you can use a longer leash (or tie two leashes together), to practice the recall with your dog at a distance.

Next, you will take the exercise off-leash, but you will only do this in a secure environment. You can do this indoors or in a fenced area, such as a backyard or dog park.

Recall Off-leash

With your dog in a secured area, let him walk around a little on his own. Then call out his name and the recall command, using your hands to tap your legs to encourage him to come toward you.

If he comes to you, crouch down and give him lots of praise.

If he is looking at you, but hesitant to come to you, act as though you are walking away, moving a few steps away from him and at the same time patting your leg and calling him again with the command.

The motion of walking away should get him to move into your direction. Crouch down when he is headed your way and praise him when he is by your side.

If he is distracted and not looking at you when you call him, clap your hands and say the word "*NO*." The sound of the clap and the "*no*" should make him look to you for direction. Now, walk a few steps backwards and pat your hand on your leg, repeat the recall command. This should get the dog to come to you. Crouch down and praise him when he gets to you.

When you recall the dog off leash, you want to make sure he comes to you and not just in your general direction. We see many people that call their dogs to them and then let the dog run past them or just come slightly in the same direction. When you recall your dog, you more than likely want to be able to put his leash back on, or get a hold of him, so make sure you teach him to come to you and stop. This is why in the beginning stages of the recall off-leash exercise, we ask that you crouch down and pet the dog, as this will condition him to come to you and be touched by you.

If the dog will not come to you off leash, go back to your on-leash exercise and practice more. We do not recommend you use any treats in the off-leash stages of the training. Condition your dog to come to you without a treat as a reward, and ensure he responds to the recall in any situation and whenever necessary.

Continue working in the secure environment until you are certain your dog is well-conditioned and responds to your recall without hesitation before allowing him to be off-leash in an unsecured area.

Dog Parks

From a traveling perspective, dog parks offer great opportunities to provide off-leash exercise for your dog. They are usually easy to find. Many communities have off-leash dog parks. We have included proper behavior in dog parks in part two of the book, as we find that many dog owners do not take their dogs to the dog park unless they are traveling. Of course, visiting a dog park is a great way to socialize your dog either on the road or at home.

At most dog parks, you will have a fenced in area with a double gate. The second gate allows you to take the leash off your dog before you enter into the off-leash area within the confines of the park. If the park offers two sections, often marked as small dogs and large dogs, please use the area that best fits your dog's size.

We recommend that you take a few moments before you enter into the park to assess the situation. Walk around the perimeter and take notice of the different dogs and their behavior. Walking around the park also makes sure your dog is calm and quiet. Do not enter the park if your dog is overly excited. Use the area outside the park to calm your dog and get him to relax.

When you enter into the gate area, take the leash off your dog and then open the gate to the park. Don't just walk in and stop; rather, walk into the park and start strolling around. You can decide, based on the energy of the other dogs, where you will go. Your dog will usually follow you or stay close to you, so walk into the area that has the dogs you want your pet to interact with.

If your dog is outgoing and plays with other dogs in the park, relax and allow him to interact. You can watch from a distance. If you feel the energy is too high or there is some posturing that might turn into a dogfight, simply call your dog to you and walk toward a different area of the park. It is never a good idea to physically pull dogs from a dog-crowded area, as this can cause a dog fight. If you have worked with your dog on the recall command, he should follow your directions and come with you, when called.

Let your dog run with the other dogs or, if there are no other dogs, walk the perimeter and let your dog explore the park. Be sure to pick up after your pet!

We usually do not recommend bringing toys to the dog park, as they can stimulate the dogs into dominating behavior. If there are no other dogs to play with, it is a good idea to throw a ball or frisbee to give your dog some added exercise.

Off leash in Unsecured Areas

There are many other off-leash opportunities, such as dog beaches or hiking trails. Please be sure that you have taught your dog the recall command and are conditioning him to come to you without fail, before you let your pet off the leash in any unsecured area.

If you ever lose sight of your dog, be sure to remain in the area where you last saw him. Dogs will usually follow their scent back to where they want to be, so if your dog gets lost or separated from you, he is most likely to return to the last spot where he was with you. So don't run off looking for him. Stay within the area and wait for him to return to you.

Chapter 11

Overnight Stays

In this chapter, we will cover some tips and exercises to make your pet a well-behaved guest, whether you stay at a campground, in a hotel or vacation rental, or spend the night at someone's home.

Whether you travel by car or RV, staying overnight with your dog will require some additional amenities. We recommend that you travel with advanced reservations for overnight accommodations, so you know where you will stop for the night. However, if you like to continue driving until you are tired and then try to locate your place to rest, your choices of accommodations might be limited. Most RV campgrounds are dog-friendly, but there are some that do not allow pets. Be prepared to be turned away, if you have not done any research or called ahead. Dog-friendly hotels are not as easy to find but there are certain hotel chains that do allow pets and it is a good idea to familiarize yourself with them prior to your travels.

We recommend advanced research while traveling with your dog. You can either use a book of campgrounds or search online. Much research can be done by cell phone while on the road. Besides your normal requirements that you have for yourself or your RV, you will want to make sure that the hotel or campground accepts dogs.

Most publications, either online or in print, will have a symbol that indicates that a place is dog-friendly. Once you find a suitable place, find out specifics about their pet policy. Some RV parks and hotels allow only smaller dogs or have restrictions on how many pets are allowed per room or per site. Many have restrictions on certain breeds. Each place is different, so don't assume, but research or call and ask about their pet policy before you get there.

Well-behaved Dogs Are Welcome

Over the years, we have stayed in many hotels, campgrounds and vacation rentals, and have interviewed owners and managers. All dog-friendly accommodations have told us that well-behaved dogs are always welcome. However, two behaviors can turn your dog into an unwelcome guest at hotels and campgrounds: excessive barking and aggressive behavior. Unfortunately, we have seen quite a bit of this type of behavior in many dogs during our travels.

Many dogs will bark when left unattended in their RV or hotel room. Most of this behavior is due to the dog being anxious and uncomfortable, or because he lacks proper exercise. If you have made sure your dog knows the RV as his secure place, you should not experience problems with him anxiously barking while he is left inside as long as you provide him with plenty of physical exercise. We will cover some additional tips for setting up the hotel room to make sure your dog is comfortable with his new surroundings.

If your dog shows aggressive behavior on the leash toward other dogs or people, it will be hard to find a welcoming campground or hotel. Once the owners have been made aware that there might be an aggressive dog on their property, they will not want to accept the liability. If your dog shows aggressiveness towards dogs or people, you will want to find a professional dog trainer to help fix the behavior. Traveling with an aggressive dog will make your travel experience very unpleasant. Just like at home, if your dog bites a human or a dog, you are responsible and liable for any medical and other damages. That is not something you want to have to worry about when you are on vacation. Consider walking your dog wearing a muzzle, until you can teach him a new behavior!

In our dog training, we frequently see that lunging at the leash and barking at other dogs or people stems from insecurity in the dog and may not be a sign of aggression. Proper leash training and showing the dog that you are in control of him and the situation will usually fix this anxious behavior.

Many dog owners are embarrassed or frustrated when they have a reactive dog that barks and lunges at a distraction. So the inclination is to quickly walk past and get away. However, failing to address the problem will only result in the behavior escalating more and more.

Refer back to Chapter 2 on proper leash training. It is essential that you have taught your dog never to pull on the leash, before you address this behavior issue!

Next, check in with yourself, making sure that you are not causing the behavior by clenching the leash tight or being afraid. We see a lot of dogs that become reactive because their owners walk them with a tight leash, or tighten up on the leash when they see another dog or distraction. Your tense grip can easily set off your dog. He feels your tension and believes that there is something from which you need protection. It is very important that you make yourself aware of your own body and reactions. Only when the handler is calm, can we expect the dog to remain calm as well.

When your dog shows his reactive behavior, practice with him by seeing this as a training opportunity. You can use the following exercise anytime. It may help you refocus your dog's reactive behavior.

Always practice with fewer distractions to start, and make sure your dog keeps the leash loose. Do not allow him to get into a highly reactive state by addressing his behavior early before it escalates. Watch his body language. When his ears go forward and he starts to focus on the distraction, redirect by either changing direction or giving a short tug on the leash. It is also possible to redirect your dog with a scent. You can have a high value treat in your closed fist and wave it in front of his nose. However, please do not actually give the treat, as the dog will see it as a reward for the behavior he is displaying. The scent is nearly meant to break his focus on the distraction. You will need to experiment with these different options to see which is most effective with your dog, or the situation at hand.

Discourage Reactive Behavior

Start by shortening the leash, so that your dog is walking by your side and not in front of you. Make sure the leash is loose. Have your arm by your side and your shoulders relaxed. Make sure you are calm.

When you walk up to a distraction, like another dog, correct your dog as soon as you see him focus on the other dog or distraction. With the use of the training collar, you can redirect his focus by giving a short and sideways pull on the leash. Use a firm "*No*" BEFORE you tug on the leash. The idea is that the "*No*" and the tug will redirect the dog. If this is not enough, change direction and walk away from the distraction. (You can also try and use the scent to redirect your dog) Work with him until his focus is back on you.

When he has calmed and is focused on walking on the loose leash, change direction again and walk back toward the distraction.

Go forward as long as he remains calm and ignores the distraction. Use the "No" and sideways tug on the leash to redirect him when he changes his focus back to the distraction. If his behavior escalates, again turn and walk away until you can get him back under control.

Disclaimer: Certainly you understand that we have no way to evaluate your individual situation, and therefore it is hard to truly address the reactive behavior within the scope of this book. If you are unable to redirect your dog on your daily walks, we highly recommend you seek out the help of a professional dog trainer to help you with this behavior issue.

Travel in a Recreational Vehicle

Long term and overnight travel in an RV with your dog can be a lot simpler than driving with your dog in a car.

A motorhome offers more room for the dog and he can walk around freely if he is conditioned properly to travel in this way. Your pet supplies are stored away nicely for the whole trip. Lunch and overnight stops are easy, as you already have your food and his food with you. Once accustomed to it, the RV is your and your dog's home away from home. In our experience, the recreational vehicle is the easiest way to travel with your dog. We have traveled with our pets for many years and for us the Recreational Vehicle is our favorite mode of travel. All our animals are at home in our Fifth Wheel. Rest stops along the way are easy and we often find the most wonderful areas along the road. We don't have to worry about shade or dog-friendly restaurants. At night, we are all sleeping in our own beds. The dogs and cat don't need to adjust to new surroundings and because of this, it is easy to leave them by themselves if we choose to go out to a nice restaurant for dinner.

Once you have selected a campground or RV park for your nightly stay, we recommend that you stop and walk Fido just prior to your arrival. Checking in and setting up the rig takes some time, and you do not want to have a restless dog, that needs to use the potty, to worry about. We always find a nice area to pull over and walk our dogs about 30 minutes before we get to our overnight destination.

Choose Your Site

Leave your dog in the car or RV while you are registering for the night. Most places will have a no pet zone in and around their office. Not everyone loves our pets like we do so we have to respect their space. There might be a pet policy that you need to sign. In most cases, you will be required to leash your dog at all times while he is outside the camper and to clean up after your dog. This is easy to follow and is just common courtesy.

Spend a little time to make sure that you get the best site for you and your pet. Most campgrounds will have different levels of campsites. You may wish to get a site that is convenient for taking your dog for a walk.

While in the office, ask about the dog amenities. Most campgrounds have some sort of dog walking area. Find out about all the areas that you can let your dog run freely to stretch his legs. Keep in mind the path you will have to take to get to the dog area. How many campsites will you have to walk around and how many dogs will be barking at you as you are walking to the dog area? Ask about other places in the RV park or nearby that you can walk your pet. If there is an area off property that you can walk your dog, consider the path that you will need to walk to get there.

Although having your site fairly close to the dog park may be convenient for you, consider that everyone with a dog will walk by your camper to get to the dog run. This could mean that your dog is constantly seeing other dogs outside the camper. If your Fido gets excited and barks a lot at other dogs, having your campsite close to the dog walking area could be a bad choice. However, you want to choose your site close enough to have a convenient walk in the middle of the night.

Never feel bad about asking to see your site first. You can either walk to the location or in some of the nicer RV parks and resorts, you might be able to get a golf cart ride to the site or sites that you can check out. If you have any questions or concerns about the campground or the RV site, ask before you leave the office. It is no fun for anyone to pull into a campsite and discover that it will not work for you. You then have to go back to the office and start looking for another site.

If you stay for a few days, you may want to see some of the local attractions while you are in the area. Ask if the park offers a pet walking service. You will read more on leaving your dog in someone's care in Chapter 13. Get names and phone numbers so that you can call and make your arrangements later.

Once you are parked in your perfect campsite, you need to set up your camper. If you haven't walked Fido for a while and somebody is traveling with you, have one person take your dog for a walk. It is a good time to explore all the dog-friendly places in the campground. Your dog is just as excited as you to have a new place to explore.

If you travel alone, get your dog settled in a little so he will not whine and bark while you are trying to get the RV set up. Take your dog for a short walk so he can do his business if he needs to. You do not need to go explore all the pet-friendly places if you are the only person available. After your dog has relieved himself you can put his bedding and some food and water next to the camper where he can see you. Make sure he is confined by his leash so he cannot run away from your campsite and is close enough that you can keep him from barking at people walking by. You can also just put him inside the camper. Just make sure he gets to go for a walk the very first thing.

After the RV is all set up you should take your dog for some exercise and explore the surroundings. Notice where you will need to walk after dark. You do not want to walk through anyone's campsite or a no-pet area. Sometimes campgrounds will not allow you to walk your dog on some grassy spots. Familiarize yourself with where you can walk your dog.

While you explore together, your dog will encounter a lot of new smells. He will want to mark to announce his presence to other dogs. Be mindful of where you allow him to do so. Don't let him pee on other campsites; rather, find the common areas that are suitable and only allow him to mark bushes and trees. Remember, pets are never allowed on children's playgrounds or around camp kitchens or common bathroom areas.

Now that you have gone for a nice walk, Fido will be good to stay in the camper while you go do human things, so go enjoy the pool or hot tub.

Hotel or Vacation Rental

You may use Hotels, Motels or Vacation homes to stay overnight for longer periods of time. This section offers some guidance on how to get the pet settled in for a stay in these new surroundings.

Of course, plan ahead and find accommodations that are pet-friendly. Be sure to ask a lot of questions and review the pet-policy of the establishment. There are several hotel chains that are pet-friendly. It is useful to know them when you find yourself traveling with no prior planning. You will be able to rely on these particular hotel chains.

When you stop for the night and you don't have any pets with you, it's easy to find a hotel that has the services and amenities you are looking for. When you travel with your dog, you will need to add more criteria to your search. Do they allow pets in their rooms? If they do, is your size pet allowed? Some establishments will have weight restrictions. For instance 25 pounds or less. Some places will not allow certain breeds and others only allow one pet per room. Do they charge you for having a pet and do they have a cleaning fee? Many hotels and vacation homes require that your dog is in a crate while in the room. Be aware that you will need to bring the crate, even if you do not use it for car travel.

If they are pet-friendly on the inside of the hotel, what do they have for your dog on the outside of the hotel? Do they have a designated dog area and is it fenced? Or is it just a green patch of grass on which you walk your dog? Maybe there are hiking trails nearby. If so, are pets allowed on the trails?

Some of these questions will be more important to you than others. Get the information before you make a reservation. If you are just going to drive and then pick a hotel when you are tired, call ahead and ask some of these questions before you arrive. You do not want to arrive at the establishment when you are tired and ready for bed to find out that they have hidden fees and charges or no dog area or even worse, they don't accept animals.

Make it a habit to stop for a walk prior to your arrival so Fido has plenty of opportunities to relieve himself and get some exercise.

Check in

When you check into your hotel, let them know that you have a pet with you. Ask for a room on the bottom floor and close to the dog exercise area. This will make your stay there much easier.

Make it your first order of business, after registering for the room, to take Fido for a walk around the area. This is important for both of you. You need to familiarize yourself with where to go for dog walks and Fido needs to sniff around and relieve himself.

Do this before you take your stuff and your dog into the hotel room. We know it is tempting to unload the car and get all settled into the room first, before you take him for a walk. However, if you take him to the room before you allow him to relieve himself, chances are he may do his business in the hallway of the hotel or in the room itself. To the dog, the hotel is unfamiliar and he may want to mark the area to advertise to other dogs that he is here now.

Explore where you can walk your dog at night. It is much better to do so now than after dark. Notice if there is a fenced in dog area. Familiarize yourself with where you can dispose of your dog bags. These are all things you want to do before you go to your room. Don't wait to try and figure this out at 2 o'clock in the morning when it is dark and cold and you are half-asleep.

Introduce the New Surroundings

After you have walked the area around the hotel and familiarized yourself with where you can walk Fido, it is time to take him to the room.

When you walk through the hotel lobby, or anywhere in the hotel, do not allow Fido to sniff around. On a short leash, with Fido next to you, walk with purpose to your room. If you stop and chat with anyone, or look at anything, make sure Fido is right near you and do not allow him to walk around sniffing.

It is tempting to open the hotel room door and let Fido off the leash to explore the new surroundings. However, it is very important that the first time you walk into a hotel room with your dog, Fido is on the leash. Don't let him just walk around the room without the leash and collar. Since the hotel is dog- friendly, there will have been plenty of dogs that have stayed in that room. Most hotels will have pet-friendly rooms that they will use only for guests with dogs, and although the hotel staff will have cleaned the room thoroughly, your dog can still pick up smells in the room.

Remember that this is not your dog's house, so going to the bathroom in here will not seem as a problem to him. Walk around the room and let him sniff around, but pay close attention. If he wants to mark a bedpost or some other item, tell him "*NO*" and redirect him.

If you are using the crate, set up the crate next to your bed. Put his bedding and toys inside the crate and leave the door open so he can go in and out. Ask him to go and lay in his crate. You can give him his favorite chew toy or bone. This way you have time to unpack and get settled in yourself.

If you do not plan on using a crate, make sure you put his bedding in an area where he can see the door and keep an eye on you. Then ask him to settle in on his dog bed or blanket. Remember to bring in the familiar items of his bedding, as this will help him feel secure and comfortable. It is also signaling him that this is his spot for the night.

As with any exercise, make this a calm event. If Fido is excited and won't settle down right away, do not pet or encourage the excited behavior. Simply wait until he is settled into his spot and then praise and pet him.

Feeding Fido

Your feeding schedule while traveling is important. Whether you are on an overnight trip or stay for longer duration, we recommend feeding your dog first thing in the morning and several hours before bedtime at night. This will give him as much time as possible to digest his food before you start traveling in the am and before you go to sleep at night. This should prevent any car sickness and travel anxiety.

You may wish to place his food and water in the bathroom. If you feed him on the carpet in the room, place a towel under his food and water. It helps keep the area clean.

We recommend you feed and water your dog for 15 minutes and then take the food bowl away. We have found that most dogs will eat little to nothing when they are in unfamiliar surroundings. If the dog won't eat at all, you can leave the food for longer periods of time. Just remember that you do not want to allow the dog to drink a lot of water, or eat right before bedtime. Most dogs will need to empty their bowels about 10-30 minutes after they eat, so be prepared to take your dog for another walk after his mealtime.

If you feel your dog is going to overeat, or the dog tends to eat his food to hasty, give him his food a little at a time.

Unless you have a puppy, you will not need to feed him in the middle of the day. However, if you are doing activities with him throughout the day, like swimming or hiking, he may need extra portions.

Leave Your Dog in the Room

You may want to go out to dinner after you are settled in and have cleaned up. We prefer to take the dogs with us, whenever possible. After dinner, if the weather is nice, we take the opportunity to walk around the area to see the town.

Your can ask the hotel staff to recommend a restaurant in the area or look up patio restaurants on your mobile device. Call ahead and make sure that Fido is welcome. Sometimes dog-friendly restaurants change their policy.

If you decide to leave your dog in the room, you will need to make sure your dog is well-behaved. If he has not been left in a hotel room by himself before, we highly recommend you leave him in his crate while you are gone. You don't want to spend all your time during dinner worrying about what your dog might be doing to the hotel room.

Take him outside for a vigorous exercise walk and to do his business just before you leave. This way you can be sure he is tired and has relieved himself.

Here are a few more things you can do to make sure he is secure and won't disturb the neighbors.

To prevent a lot of barking while you are gone, provide some background noise so he cannot hear other people walking up and down the hotel corridors. Most dogs bark because they hear someone outside the room. We found tuning the radio on a talk show works well. If you use the TV, make sure it is not a channel with a lot of shooting or blowing stuff up noises. That might be scary. Choose talk shows over music. It just works better. Another option is to run the fan in the bathroom. These fans are usually pretty loud and can provide some white noise for your dog.

If your dog is not kept inside a crate while in the hotel room, be sure he cannot see outside the windows. If he sees people walking or other dogs or birds, he will likely bark at them. You can sometimes move a table or chair in front of the window so that he is unable to reach it. Put a towel on the bottom of the door so he cannot see shadows in the hallway.

If you want to confine your dog while you are gone because you are afraid he will do damage to the hotel room, you must travel with a dog crate. Do not lock the dog in the bathroom of your room! The small tiled room is a very scary place for a dog and provides no comfort for him. Leave him in his crate, with his familiar bedding and toys. If you lock him into the bathroom, he will likely dig at the door and tear up the floor.

We highly recommend you leave the room and stay just outside for a few minutes to ensure Fido is not making a huge ruckus that everyone will hear. Remember, if he is barking and won't settle in, you must find another option for your dinner plans. Leaving a noisy barking dog in a room is unacceptable.

A little trick that you can use is to give him a "special" treat just before you leave. That special treat should be a type of chew food. This will keep him occupied for quite a while. Only use your "special" treat when you are leaving him alone. When you return back to the room, pick up the "special" bone and put it away and then put your dog on a leash and collar and take him outside for a walk.

Frequent Walks

While overnight in hotels, you need to walk the dog more frequently than normally at home. This is because you are in a strange place, and even a good dog that has had plenty of housebreaking training can be tempted to relieve himself in the room.

Before you go to sleep at night, place your leash and collar and a flashlight near your bedside and have a pair of shoes and clothing ready to put on. This leaves you fully prepared when the dog needs to go outside in the middle of the night. It is no fun trying to find all of that in the dark and when you're half asleep.

You may trust your dog will wake you up if he needs to go to the bathroom, or set your alarm to wake you sometime during the night to take your dog for a walk.

Get dressed and ready to go outside before you talk to your dog. For all he knows, you might just get up to go to the bathroom yourself. Just because you got out of bed does not mean he gets to go outside. After you are ready to go, grab the leash and collar, use your command for "*outside*" and exit through the hotel area in a purposeful walk. Again, do not let Fido sniff inside the hallways of the hotel.

Do not walk around a lot or play with him. This is just a potty break, so go directly to the area where he can relieve himself. If you have trained him to use the bathroom on command, use your command now. When he is done, pick up after him if needed and go back to your room.

When you get back to the room, put him back on his dog bed or inside the crate. Do not give him lots of attention. When you pet him or talk a lot, he will not want to go back to sleep, so if you yourself wish to get more sleep, keep things calm and just expect him to settle back in and go back to bed yourself.

When you wake up in the morning, make it your first order of business to walk the dog. You do not want to walk around the hotel room, after you have awakened, and sip coffee. He will need to go to the bathroom when he wakes up just like you do. So don't be tempted to make a cup of coffee or watch TV while laying in bed.

After you take him for his morning walk, feed and water him. While he is eating and drinking, you can get ready for the day. If you plan on eating breakfast within walking distance of the room, take him with you to a dog friendly restaurant, or place him in the crate just before you leave for breakfast, following the same routine you used before.

You can leave him in the room while packing the car, or someone can take him outside for some exercise. If you put him in the car while you are getting ready, he is going to be very nervous. After you have loaded up the vehicle, walk your dog one last time before you start your trip.

Spending Time at a Friend's House

Many times while traveling across the states, we got the opportunity to stop and visit a dear friend or a family member. Of course they are always welcoming to us and our dogs. However, when you bring your dogs into someone's home, it is always more challenging than traveling with them otherwise. When someone opens their home to you, you want your dogs on their very best behavior. So we like to address some of the things that could be challenging for you and your dog.

Arrival

Upon your arrival at the home, you might be tempted to fling open your car door and let your dog run freely to meet the other family. Ensure you are in control of your dog, especially when you are going into a home with other dogs or with children. Don't put undue stress on your family or friend.

When you first arrive at the house, leave your dog in the car if possible. Leave the AC running or some windows rolled down, depending on the weather conditions. Remember to put on the emergency brake. It will take a lot of stress off of both parties when you take the time to greet each other without the dog at first.

If you are not comfortable with leaving the dog in the car, put him on a leash and walk him up to the family and meet them outside the home. Make sure he has time to relieve himself after the travel before entering the house!

When you first introduce strangers to your dog, it is best to have him outside the car. Ask everyone to ignore the dog. You do not want people to go right up to your dog and grab him. You want your dog to walk up to the people. Allow your dog to take in the smell of everyone without any interaction. Just have him on the leash with you and have a conversation with your friends.

If he comes right up to the people and is not afraid, they can acknowledge your dog, as long as the dog is not hyper. Many dogs get very excited when they meet other people. If this is the case with your dog, you don't want to give him too much attention at the arrival, or he will be very excited and hard to control.

A timid dog may back away from someone. Ask them not to go after him, or crouch down. Just have them ignore the dog. You must let your dog approach the people on his terms. If he is not warming up to them, start walking together towards the house. Ask the person to pay no attention to the dog. You do not want him off the leash until he has accepted the people and the new surroundings. If he is timid, keep him near you. Sit down and talk about your travels and visit while your dog is still on the leash next to you. After he has acknowledged and sniffed the people and walked away from them, it is okay to release your dog and let him run around a secure area.

If you cannot let the dog in a fenced back yard, leave him on the leash while you get the tour of the house. Find out what the new surroundings are and where the dog is allowed and where not.

Introduction to Other Pets

Introduce other pets living in the home to your dog upon your arrival. If possible, introduce other dogs outside the home. Walk your dog up to the new dog in a neutral area and let them sniff each other. Once they are comfortable with each other continue to the backyard or the house. Supervise both dogs closely for a while, as they get acquainted further.

If the two dogs start to growl at each other, you will need to spend more time with the getting-acquainted process. The best way to get this done is to go for a walk. You do not want to do this in the backyard. Walk around neutral ground. Take a walk down the road. Choose an area that is neutral territory for both dogs. This way they do not feel the need to protect their territory.

Introduction to Another Dog

Ask your friend to handle their dog while you handle yours. With both dogs leashed, start the walk down a sidewalk side by side, but separated by about 10 to 15 feet. The important thing here is that you continue to move. Do not stop and let the dogs focus on each other. When you are walking together do not talk to your dogs. Talk among the humans and just walk. Start the walk separated by 10 to 15 feet, then gradually make the distance shorter, but only if the dogs are not focused on each other. As you walk and talk, gradually get closer to each other. If one dog starts to growl at the other, correct the dog and hold that distance. Continue to walk. Soon they will lose interest. It is very important that you do not stop moving. If you stop moving, the dogs will focus on each other. When you are moving, they will have to focus on walking down the road. Continue walking until everyone is walking side-by-side. Watch their body language and as they relax, you can shuffle around until the two dogs are walking side-by-side and ignoring each other. Once you return to the house and the dogs are still good, stop outside the driveway and continue talking. Now you can let the dogs sniff each other. Usually, a dog's reaction towards other dogs is caused by the handler, so be sure to have the leashes loose and without tension. After you have stood outside the driveway for a few minutes and you are comfortable that everything is good, you can head to the backyard and release your dogs to play. If you are not totally comfortable, you can continue walking and talking in the backyard until you are comfortable to release the dogs. Release them at the same time and let them go play. It may be best to keep them separated, unless supervised.

Inside the Home

Before you let your dog inside the house, talk to your friends about any boundaries or places where your dog is not allowed. If there are areas that are off limits to your dog, discuss how you will keep him out of those areas. Hopefully, you can just close the doors for the remainder of the visit. Most dogs in a strange environment will want to stay with their owner whenever possible.

Even if your dog gets along fine with the other pets in the home, we recommend that you pick up all of the toys and food around the house. You do not want any fighting or defending of food or toys inside.

Decide where he will be sleeping for the night and where you will want him to hang out throughout the day. Put his bedding or blanket in the area of the house in which you will want him to sleep. If your host allows your dog to be in your bedroom, put his bedding close to where you will sleep. Remember, his bedding is the only familiar and comfortable place he has in the house. If you really want to make his bed a comfortable place, you can put a shirt that you have been wearing on his bed.

Find out where you can feed him. If there are other pets in the home, we highly recommend you feed your dogs in a separate area, away from the other pets. You can have them share water, but do not feed them close to each other.

If the home has a backyard and a dog door, make sure you spend a few moments showing your dog how to use it.

Dog Etiquette

When you have your dog staying at someone's house, you don't always think of the strain it puts on the household. They have their own routine that they go through every day: when they take their dog outside, what and when they feed him, what toys their dog gets to play with and so forth. Your host will be focused on making everyone happy and relaxed the whole time that you are staying with your dog. So you want to make the visit as stress-free as possible. These are some tips and ideas you might consider when visiting with your dog at someone's house:

- Be aware of the rules and boundaries your host has for their dog and try to have your dog follow the same rules. If you allow your dog on your couch at home, but the host family does not, you should immediately instruct your dog that he is not allowed on the furniture here.

- If the dogs want to play, you will want to have them outside so you don't have to worry about them getting excited and jumping on the furniture or jumping on a person or breaking something.

- When your dog goes to the bathroom, you should just go and scoop it up and dispose of it. Most dogs will have an area that they like to use to go to the bathroom in their yard. But your dog does not have any preference and he will go to the bathroom anywhere in the yard, because it is not his yard.

- Make sure that your dog is always under control even if their dog is not. If your dog is super excited, put him on his leash and collar and have him stay next to you. Get him to settle down before you allow him to roam around.

- Offer to take the host dog along for your walks. Walking both dogs together frequently will increase their bond with each other.

- Use your dog's toys for both dogs to play with. You do not want the host family to have to replace their toys after you have left. If they want to put down their dog's favorite toy, make sure that your dog does not bully it away from him.

- You do not want your dog to intimidate or bully the host dog while you are there. It might not seem like a big deal that your dog is bullying the host dog and that you are glad it is not your dog that is the one that is submissive. We can assure you that the owners of the host dog will not appreciate seeing their dog being bullied even if no one is getting hurt. If you see your dog bullying the host dog, you need to stop it quickly. Again, if you have to, put your dog on a leash and collar and keep him with you.

Chapter 12

Travel Diet

Feed your dog the same food on the road that you feed at home. Don't experiment with diet or vitamins on the road. Make your dietary changes prior to traveling. This is also why we recommend you take enough food to get you through your travel time, or ensure you feed a dog food that is readily available throughout the area you are traveling in. There is already a lot of anxiety that comes with taking the dog out of his usual surroundings, and changing his diet would only add to his discomfort. As you travel with your dog, you may not give much thought to feeding him. You put the dog in the car, get to where you are going, feed the dog, and do it again the next day. However, travel is very exciting to most dogs and new and unfamiliar surroundings can often lead to an upset stomach or digestive issues.

Although no change in food is needed, you should structure your dog's feeding schedule according to your travel time. This will make your dog more comfortable, help with potty breaks, and make it a lot less likely for him to have any accidents in unfamiliar places.

Here are some ideas to help you with preparations before you go on your trip. We already mentioned that you need to bring along his food and water dish, any treats, and chew foods (raw hides, etc.) that you use at home. Use these familiar items to help him stay more at ease in the unfamiliar surroundings.

We have found that a plastic tub with locking or tight fitting lid is the best way to store dog food. You can also store the bowls, treats, and chew toys in the same container. You want it large enough that you can put enough food in it so it will last your pet through the traveling process. This is also a great way to prevent the dog food from spilling all over the car or RV.

Be mindful of where that container will be placed in your travel vehicle. Try to make it readily accessible as you travel down the road. When you stop for lunch, you can give some water to your pet while you are eating. After he has had a break, just pick up everything and throw it back in the container and put the container away.

Put your dog on a regular feeding schedule when you travel. This will be loosely based on the type of travel you do. How many hours will you travel or stay in one place?

We recommend that you feed and water your dog the very first thing in the morning after his morning walk. You may have to get up a little earlier than usual for this routine but it will make your travel day a lot easier. If you try to feed the dog while everyone is getting ready for the road, your dog may not eat. Especially if he is a bit sensitive, all the hustle will get him feeling uneasy and he may not eat. If you see this, make sure you allow some time before you pack up everything, so that he can eat quietly without feeling rushed. This will also give him time to digest the food and water a little before you take him for one more walk.

The other extreme we see on the road are dogs that will scarf down the food and then vomit it all up. This is a sign of travel anxiety in the animal. It is important to create a calm, nurturing atmosphere. If you have open suitcases and start packing up everything, your dog may become anxious about whether you are going to take him with you. In his anxious state he hurries his eating and gets an upset stomach. We suggest you stay nearby where he can see you. If you leave to have breakfast and he is left alone, it may only increase his travel anxiety.

Feed him while calmly sitting nearby. Maybe you can enjoy your morning cup of coffee and eat some breakfast. Just enjoy the morning, talk to your family, make some calls or check your email.

As long as he does not binge eat, give him all the food and water that he wants for about 15 minutes. If your dog tends to overeat, feed him what you think is the appropriate amount, but let him have all the water that he wants.

Once your dog has finished eating and drinking, prepare for the day's travel. Pick up the dog food and take the water away. Continue packing for the road trip. If you can, keep your dog in a confined area before you travel.

Before everyone loads into the car or the camper to start the day's travel, take your dog for one more potty-walk. If you wait until you already loaded all the bags and others are already in the car ready to go, Fido might be too excited to go to the bathroom.

Put him on his leash and collar and walk him to a designated dog walking area. This is not playtime so don't bring a tennis ball or a stick. You want your dog to do his business before you start traveling. Bringing a toy will make him think it's playtime rather than about going to the bathroom. If you have a dog run area or a place that is secure, you can let him off leash there and the smells will induce going to the bathroom. Monitor whether your dog does a number one or a number two. This will determine if you need to stop again in about one or two hours. After your dog has done his business, load him into the vehicle and continue your travel.

Even though this book is about traveling with your pet, nutrition is something very important that we would like to cover. Hopefully you can use this information in your everyday life as well as while traveling.

Examine the bag of dog food that you feed your pet now. Look at the ingredients on the back of the bag. Find the section on the bag that says "ingredients." The benefit of this list is that manufacturers are required to list ingredients from the most quantity down to the least in the dog food. This makes it very easy to see the quality of ingredients in the dog food. We want you to look at the first couple of ingredients. The main ingredient in the food will be the very first one listed. Good dog food will have either a meat, fish, or vegetable listed as the first ingredient. Corn as the first ingredient is not a good sign, since corn is merely a filler ingredient and has no nutritional value.

When Jim first started his boarding kennel, he thought that all dog food was the same. He would buy the least expensive dog food that he could find. Jim would have up to 50 dogs that he would feed twice a day and he wanted to keep his food bill down as much as possible. When it came time to clean the kennels, there was always a lot of dog waste. At some point, Jim hired a Kennel Manager who was very interested in dog nutrition and had taken a few classes on the topic. The first thing she recommended was to change the diet for all the dogs. She showed Jim the ingredients of the dog food that he was currently using. The first two ingredients were corn and corn meal. Then she showed him the ingredients of the food she wanted to use, which were chicken and chicken by-products. She explained that the food would cost a little bit more, but the dogs would look and feel a lot better, and the dog waste would be significantly less. Jim was a little skeptical, especially since the food bill would increase, but he decided to experiment on four of his own dogs. At the time, Jim had eight personal protection Rottweilers that he was training and selling. Jim would feed four of them the new dog food. In the first couple of days, the first thing he noticed was the decrease in waste. For the four dogs eating the new dog food, Jim could clean up the waste with a pooper scooper. All the other dogs continued to have lots of loose waste in their dog runs. Jim had to clean their kennels by spraying them out with a water hose, the way he had always done in the past. After two weeks, he noticed the coats on the four dogs were shiny with no dandruff. Compared to the rest of the dogs, the four looked healthier. Jim was sold! Needless to say, he started feeding the new dog food to all the dogs in the kennel. To this day, Jim will only buy premium dog food. The brand name is not as important as the ingredients used in the dog food. Always check the ingredients used before you purchase the dog food.

Other things you will notice on the labels are the percentage of vitamins in the dog food. The percentages of vitamins are important. We know you want to know what you are ingesting with your diet, and the same should be true for your pets. The easiest way to match the correct food to your dog's needs is to use the label. The label for the dog food should match with the type of dog you have. For instance, if you are raising a puppy, you would want to get puppy food in the brand of food that you like. If you have an older dog, you'll want to get food for senior dogs. If you have a working dog, get food for the working or sporting breed, which may be labeled for active dogs. The different types of food are specifically formulated for life stages or activity levels; for example, protein will be higher for puppies and lower for senior dogs.

When changing dog food, especially when upgrading the quality of your dog food, don't mix the foods together. Most people will tell you to gradually mix in the new with the old food, but that is not necessarily the best way to change. Either use up the rest of the food that you have or just throw it out before you change the dog food. If you're not sure the dog food will work, buy a small bag. When you switch the food, use up the full bag before making any decision. If the food works for you, use all of it. If it doesn't work, try another five pounds of a different type of food. Feed the full five pounds before making any decisions.

There is less to worry about when changing from low-quality to high-quality dog food. The pet will better digest the high-quality food and have more energy. Changing from high-quality food to low-quality food may give the pet a harder time digesting, resulting in loose stool. This will mean more waste to clean up.

If you would really want to make sure that your pet is receiving all the nutrition that he needs, try adding some wheat germ oil. Wheat germ oil is a super premium oil that contains many good vitamins and oils that your pet will love. You only need to use one cap full and pour directly over the dry dog food and then mix it in. For smaller dogs, use a lesser amount. Be aware that dogs really like the taste of the oil and may have a tendency to eat more food than usual. You can usually find wheat germ oil at local feed stores. There are other oils that are similar to this, providing the Omega 3 and Omega 6 fatty acids. They are just as wonderful. We have used wheat germ oil on all our dogs with great results.

There are two things that you will need to be aware of if you want to change dog food; dog food allergies and dog food intolerance. First, dog food allergies are just that, allergies to some ingredients in the dog food. Some signs of food allergies may be constant itchy skin to chronic ear infections. Although food allergies are not as serious to your pet, they cause discomfort and should be dealt with quickly. If we have a dog that is allergic to a particular ingredient in the dog food, we usually just change the dog food to a different ingredient. For instance, if we think the beef in the dog food is causing the allergy, we might switch to a turkey based dog food with no beef or even use a vegetarian dog food.

Second, dog food intolerance is where the digestive system is unable to handle an ingredient in the dog food. This is a little bit more serious because it might cause vomiting or diarrhea. Change your dog food immediately!

Talk to your veterinarian if at any time you have any concerns about food allergies, food intolerance, or if you just want more information.

Chapter 13

Leave Fido in Someone's Care

Throughout your travel, you will spend a lot of time with your dog, but there may be a few occasions when you will need to go without him. Some of these times are short; for example, you will go to a grocery store to pick up some items, or you may go out to a nice restaurant for dinner that won't allow dogs. Other times you may want to go to a local attraction like a museum or amusement park, where dogs are not allowed. Even if you do not plan to go anywhere without your dog, it is important to consider what you would do if you had to leave him in case of an emergency.

Leaving your pet by himself for a few hours will be no problem if he is comfortable and has had plenty of exercise. We have discussed this in previous chapters. You can leave the radio or TV on for some background noise, as this will prevent him from hearing other people or dogs outside the RV or hotel room. Give him his special treat and he will be entertained until you return.

Make sure the dog is comfortable inside the room or RV. Provide for ventilation or air-conditioning while you are gone.

As of now, we live in our Fifth Wheel approximately six months out of the year. When we leave our dogs in our camper, we leave the air conditioner on as if we were still in the camper. Or we leave our roof fan on and the windows open for air ventilation when AC is not needed. If you plan on leaving your pet in your camper, make sure the temperature is just as comfortable as when you are there with him.

Leave for a Day Trip

When you plan to be away for longer periods of time, consider what you want to do with Fido. If you travel in a RV, you can find someone that will come and take your dog out for a walk while you are gone.

If you are not sure if your dog will bark when you leave the camper, you should test him before you go on your road trip. Exercise your dog with a good 30 minute walk before you try this. Set the camper up in the same way you would when you are ready to leave for your day trip, and go outside of the camper and wait nearby. You don't want to sit in a chair nearby, as your dog will surely sense that you are just outside the camper. You may go as far as getting into your car and driving to the visitor parking and then walking back to the camper. You can go spend half an hour at the pool and then come back. This will allow you to know how your dog will act when you are gone for longer periods of time.

If he barks a couple of times in the first few minutes, don't do anything. Sometimes the dog will bark just to express his disagreement with you leaving without him. Remember he is safe and hopefully he will lie down in a few minutes and wait for your return.

Doing this little test before you go on your road trip will give you a piece of mind that he is not barking and disturbing the neighbors.

If he does continue to bark in the camper then you will have to come up with an alternative other than him staying by himself.

If he continues to bark for a long time, you will have to go back in the camper. You cannot punish him in any way. He will either feel safe and comfortable in the camper and go to sleep, or he will not feel comfortable and safe in the camper and he will bark. You do not want to find out that your dog is barking in the camper by the campground calling you. Do this test before you leave so everyone can enjoy the trip.

Destructive Behavior

We have had hotel managers tell us stories about dogs destroying rooms when they were left alone in the room. Destructive behavior usually comes from fear or anxiety. It has nothing to do with the dog being upset or mad. He is left in a strange place and the people that keep him safe are not there. So you will want to redirect his mind with something that is comfortable and calming to him. Because you do not live in the hotel, nothing smells familiar. This is why it is so important that you have his familiar bedding and some of his toys.

We recommend you use the crate and leave him crated while you are away from your room if you know your dog has shown destructive behavior in the past. He is secure in the crate and will not be able to destroy the furnishings.

Another reason why dogs become destructive is for lack of exercise. It is possible that you are not providing the dog with enough opportunity to release his pent up energy. He has to get rid of his energy somehow. How much exercise a dog needs largely depends on his temperament. If he is a high energy dog, he needs more exercise than a medium or low energy dog. This isn't necessarily something that is breed related. In every breed, there are high, medium and low energy dogs.

Potty Breaks

Now you will have to decide if he will need to go to the bathroom during the time that you are gone. You will probably already know how long he is able to go without going to the bathroom and you will probably adjust your trip accordingly. But please keep in mind that something unexpected might occur. There is always a chance you will be unable to return in the time you prepared for. Most people will think that's not going to happen. You will need to consider the unexpected before you leave your dog by himself. What if you have vehicle problems and are physically unable to drive back? What if you are in a traffic accident or worse yet, someone has to go to the hospital? Have a plan in place for this worst case scenario.

If you travel with an RV, the easiest solution is to have a "hide-a-key" outside of the camper that will always remain there in case you need to have someone get into your camper while you are away. Even though it takes a little time to get set-up, you may find other reasons you are glad you have spare keys hidden somewhere outside of your camper. Putting it in a small container and placing it hidden in a storage bin of your camper is the easiest thing to do. The next time you go to the hardware store, just make some key copies of your camper and hide them outside. It is not a bad idea to have extra keys in case someone locks the camper while the keys are inside. Let the camp hosts know you will be gone and leave your cell number in case someone needs to contact you. It will give you piece of mind knowing your dog will be taken care of no matter what.

Dog Walkers

Dog walkers in RV parks are usually a hidden gem most people don't know about. These folks live or work at the park, and for a small fee, will take your dog for a walk while you are out having fun.

Usually, this service is not published anywhere so you will have to ask the counter personnel if there is someone that can walk your pet. The campground understands very well how many people travel with their pets and that they will offer a service that will help the whole family enjoy their stay at the RV Park. Having a "dog walker" take care of your pet while you are on a day trip is usually the simplest and safest way to have your dog taken care of while you are away.

Dog walkers from the RV Park will only walk your dog within the park.

If you feel comfortable enough, you will discuss either leaving your camper open or giving that person a key to your camper. Make sure it is clear between both parties how often they will walk your dog and how much they charge. It is important that you have them stop by prior to your day trip to make sure your dog can be introduced to them. Let them know if you want them to water or feed your dog as well as walk him.

If the campground does not offer a dog walking service, search for a pet service in the nearby town. Even if there is not a specific dog walking service listed, call some dog grooming businesses or other pet care services and ask if they offer dog walking or ask them to recommend someone that can come out to your RV park. Do not feel bad about asking for this service. That is the simplest and safest for your pet. Most pet services will be more than happy to try to assist you and your pets needs.

Dog Daycare

Dog daycare services are usually a home environment that will watch pets throughout the day. They focus on your pet being able to roam freely in their secure area. As the name suggests, they focus on your pet staying just for the day. Each daycare service is different and they will offer different services for you and your pet. When interviewing a dog daycare, make sure you ask a lot of questions. Do they have a pickup and delivery service to and from your RV? Do they offer the dog food or do you bring your own? Do they check the shot records for all dogs before they come in? What are their operating hours, and how much does it cost if you show up late to pick up your pet?

Before you use one of these facilities, you have to make absolutely sure that your dog gets along with other dogs and that he will not try to escape.

Some daycare centers offer pet grooming and other pet care services you can choose from while the dog is there. Make time before you take your trip and take a tour of the facility. Be certain it does live up to the advertisement and that you get a good feel that your pet will be well taken care off.

Overnight Stays

If you plan to stay one or more days away from your pet, you will want a more secure and structured environment for him. Pet walking services do not mind walking your dog throughout the day, but it is much harder to find someone that will walk him outside of normal business hours. So you will need to find another alternative to a walking or day care service.

For overnight stays or for dogs that do not get along with others, a boarding kennel is the best option. Most towns will have some sort of Boarding Kennel. If you plan to stay away overnight this may be the only option for your pet. Some Day Care places offer overnight stays as well. These are a little less stressful because your dog will be in a home environment and possibly have other pets to play with. Some facilities will have better amenities for the dogs than most hotels will have for humans. And that is not a bad thing for either the human or the dog because you can feel comfortable that your dog is having as much fun as you are having.

Boarding Kennel or Pet Resort

These facilities are made to be extremely safe and secure for all types of pets. When you drop off your pet at a boarding kennel, you need not worry about his safety. The run your dog will stay in will be completely enclosed so that he cannot get to any other dogs and other dogs are unable to get to him. He will not be able to climb over or out of the enclosure. Some boarding kennels will have indoor and outdoor runs. Others will be only indoors. If need be, they will be heated or air-conditioned to a very comfortable temperature for the dogs. They will have structured feeding times and most facilities will offer exercise time for your dog.

Boarding facilities are built for the safety of your dog. You do not need to worry if he likes to bark or run away or jump fences or beat up on other dogs or people. However if he does have some of those tendencies, do let the facility know so that the kennel attendants will be extra cautious.

Ask for a tour. You can inspect the facility before you drop him off and ask questions while you are there. Some boarding kennels may offer a pickup and delivery service. You can request additional services such as play time and grooming services. Don't forget to have copies of your vaccine record.

When Jim had his boarding kennel, he offered "play time" for the pets if the owner wanted it. If the owner wanted the extra play time, Jim would ask very specifically if the dog had tendencies to climb or jump over fences. In the years that Jim had his boarding kennel, only one dog jumped over his 6-foot fence. Fortunately, he was just chasing a stray cat that he had seen on the other side of the fence. The cat just climbed up a tree and Jim was able to go over and put the dog back on the leash and bring him back into the kennel and all was well. When the owner came to pick up his dog Jim told him what had happened. Then he told Jim that his dog had jumped his fence before at his home, but did not think that he could get over Jim's fence. He was afraid Jim would not want to board his dog if he knew he was a fence jumper. Fortunately, everything turned out okay. Jim would have just not offered "Play Time" to this dog had Jim known that he was a fence jumper.

Board at the Attraction

Sometimes larger tourist attractions offer boarding facilities while you are visiting. This can be a good solution when you are only staying for a few hours. Such a boarding facility will be open as long as the attraction is open. Usually, this is a safe place to keep your dog. They usually require a copy of your dog's vaccines and you may want to bring a padlock to put on the gate. If you have multiple dogs they can stay together. If you want to bring bedding and toys and other things for your dog, remember that it might get soiled or stained while he is there. The boarding facilities are usually right at the main entrance. Leave your contact information and a copy of his vaccines. Usually no one will interact with your dog the whole time that he is there.

Once you walk away from him, he will settle in and wait for you to return. If you return he will expect that you are coming to get him, so don't come by to check on him. Just enjoy the time in the park knowing that your dog is safe and will be there when you are ready. Once you have finished your stay in the park, you can go get your dog and head off to your next adventure.

However, if your stay at the attraction is long, you will need to come and walk your dog, unless you want him to do his business inside the enclosure. When you take him for the walk, make sure you spend some time with him. Take him for a nice walk, not just to go potty, but also to exercise and interact with him.

Chapter 14

All Aboard!

One of our favorite ways to vacation is near or on water. Jim has been a boater since early childhood and has owned some kind of boat throughout his life. We have spent many weekends on our own boats, a pontoon boat and a speedboat, and we have vacationed on several houseboats. In addition, we have been able to find a few harbor cruises that allowed dogs.

Traveling on board a ship or boat is very different than traveling by car. Bringing your pet will require that you prepare him and plan your route accordingly to his needs.

Whether you own your own vessel or rent one, or even if you take a cruise, Fido must first be accustomed to the way a boat feels, and to all the different sounds and smells that come with traveling on water.

We highly recommend getting your dog used to water prior to getting him on board. If possible, spend a few afternoons near a lake or on the beach. Allow your dog to take in the smells and play in the water. If you have been traveling with your dog for a while, he is now used to going into different surroundings with you. You have formed a bond that has him trust you and he will be comfortable by your side.

If your dog is not a very good swimmer, consider getting him a life jacket. They are easily found at many pet stores or online.

Find our favorite dog travel accessories at our website at ModernCanineServices.com.

Get Fido On-board

As with vehicle travel, it is always best to give your dog the opportunity to get on-board on his own four paws. However, this is more difficult with a boat that is bouncing around the water than with a vehicle sitting still.

If the boat is docked, walk Fido on-leash to the boat and have him hop in on this own, if possible. If the dog is small or otherwise unable to jump into the boat on his own, you can help him get on-board, but try to let the dog move his own legs. For example, you may lift the dog's front legs onto the boat and then let him stand there and gently lifting his hindquarters, allow him to move into the boat. We use a ramp for our dogs to get in and out of the boat.

Once the dog is aboard the vessel, let him find his sea-legs. The boat will be moving with the waves, gently rocking back and forth. Just sit in a chair and let your dog get comfortable with this movement. He may just stand there wide-legged or he may lay down.

If he wants to explore, walk around with him. We do not recommend you let him off-leash this early in the process. We have seen many dogs just jump off the boat and into the water. To keep him safe, keep him leashed.

As with any other travel vehicle, your dog should have a place he can be without being in the middle of the aisle. Arrange a towel for him to lay on. We recommend a towel instead of his dog bed, as boat adventures usually involve playing in or around water. When we boat with our dogs, Heidi and Jaeger, the smaller Jack Russell, Heidi, gets to sit up in the bow with Birgit. We place a towel there for her and she is happy to sit in the front with her nose up in the wind. The large Chessy, Jaeger, likes to lay in the aisle right near the driver's seat. There is no room for such a large dog to fit into the legroom in front of the passenger seating, so the aisle is the only place for him.

Dogs can get sea-sick, so make his first trip short. Provide shade or keep him cool by letting him swim, if he likes it, so he does not overheat on your boat trip.

Houseboats and Cabin Cruisers

We rented houseboats on Lake Powell and other lakes several times. Our dogs loved being in the front patio area during most of the driving time and moved around the boat freely when we were anchored. They quickly accustomed themselves and were comfortable. If you own your own boat, it will take only a few trips to get your dog fully situated and he will enjoy the boat vacation. If you plan to rent the boat, as we often did, be sure to research and call ahead. Most rental places will have certain boats that are dog-friendly and others that are not. Ask a lot of questions so you are sure your dog is welcomed.

To get the dog accustomed to the boat, you should use a similar approach as described for RV travel in Chapter 6. You can use the treats, spread around the interior, to help your dog explore and associate the boat with a pleasant experience. Similar to RV travel, traveling in a houseboat or cruiser will come with a lot of smells and noises. It is ideal to have the dog get used to the boat on the trailer, out of the water, if at all possible. If this is not an option, allow the dog to be on-board while the boat is docked first and let him get comfortable.

Cruise Ships and Boat Cruise

There are a few commercial cruises that will allow dogs on their ships. When you bring your dog, he must be leashed. Make sure he has had a good walk for exercise and time to relieve himself, prior to the trip. Realize that you may just have to sit and not be able to move around as freely as you would without a dog. Hopefully, you have another person with you, so someone can stay with the dog at all times, as there is no way to leave him unattended when you want to use the restroom, or go inside to order food or drinks during the trip.

On vacation cruises, pets are not welcomed. There are currently no major cruise lines that are dog-friendly. Service dogs are an exception, but even Therapy dogs are not permitted on the big cruise ships, and they do not allow service dogs in training. However, if you travel in Europe, or other parts of the world, there are often times river cruises or ferries that allow pets. It is always best to call ahead or research online for the most current information.

One British cruise line offers voyage from New York to England, with a kennel on board for your pet. Your dog will not travel with you in your cabin, but at least he is on board with you for the trip and you can visit him at the kennel area.

Chapter 15

Can Fido Fly?

If you plan to travel by airplane, either within the US or abroad, you will need to do a lot more research before your travels. Especially when you leave the country and travel internationally, you will need to specifically look up the countries' regulations on bringing in live animals. Each country has its own regulations which can change from time to time, so make sure you check each time you plan to visit a foreign country.

In addition to vaccinations and legal paperwork that may be required for your dog to enter into another country, you also have to research your flight route carefully. Each airline has its own unique regulations in regards to pets traveling, so it is imperative, even if you travel within the US, to do your research. Many airlines that allow dogs limit the number of animals per flight, so it is a good idea to make your reservations early and to let the airline know that you are bringing your dog with you.

In general, your dog's weight will largely determine how he will travel. So before you start your conversations with the airline make sure you know your dog's exact weight and size.

Airlines that allow dogs in the main cabin usually restrict them to small dogs, that can travel in a carry-on bag. We have specific information for you in this chapter on both, dogs that can travel in the cabin and dogs that will need to travel in the cargo hold.

Find out from your airline which way your dog can travel. Once you know this, you will need to purchase the "airline approved" crate or carry-on bag.

Dogs Traveling in the Cabin

While every airline has different regulations, generally speaking, pets who weigh less than 20 pounds - pet carrier weight included - can travel in the cabin if the airline permits it. A soft or hard case pet carrier must securely fit under the seat in front of you and is counted as one of your carry-ons. When you look to purchase your pet carrier, be sure to verify that it is airline approved. You can go to our website at ModernCanineServices.com and check out our recommended products in the travel essentials section.

If your pet meets your airline's criteria for traveling in the cabin, this is probably the best option for him.

Spending Time in the Pet Carrier

Keep in mind that your dog must remain in the carrier for the entire flight. Your dog may whine or bark when confined in the carrier, especially when he can see you and is unsure why is his inside. We highly recommend that you get your dog used to the carrier weeks ahead of travel. You can use the exercises in chapter 4 to get him accustomed to the carrier.

After the initial crate training, make sure to have your dog spend time in the carrier while you carry him around. To practice, take him to restaurants or into stores with you. Practice with him staying in the crate for several hours at a time, since that will be the case during your flight time.

You can put a worn t-shirt in the bag with him, so he has your familiar smells with him to be comfortable.

Before you go on your flight, feed your pet 2 hours before the flight and then limit his food and fluid intake, so he will not need to go potty and won't get motion-sick. You can talk to your veterinarian and see if the vet recommends a sedative for your dog to calm him during the travel time. If your dog is carrier-trained prior to the flight, he should be fine.

Make sure you have his pet passport, or other documentation required. Have the dog collar with his ID tag on the dog and his leash handy, in case you want or need to take him out.

Security Checkpoint

After you have checked in for your flight, you and your dog will need to go through the airport security checkpoints.

You have two options to take your dog through the screening process. You can take him out of the carrier, and have the empty pet carrier go through the X-Ray belt, while you walk through the body scanner with your dog on-leash. Or you can leave your dog in the pet carrier and walk through the body scanner with him in it. If you leave him in the bag, TSA officials may ask to inspect the bag after you have been scanned.

To simplify the process, we recommend you have only a few other carry-on items with you, so you have your hands free to handle the dog and the carrier.

In-flight

After boarding the aircraft, you can store the pet carrier under the seat right away, or keep the dog with the carrier on your lap until the flight attendants clear the cabin for take-off.

During the flight, you may want to interact with your dog. You can have the carrier on your lap during the flight, but your dog must remain contained in the carrier at all times. If you are tempted to open the carrier to give your dog a treat or pet him, do so carefully and only open the bag a little bit. You can give your dog a small ice cube, but again, don't overdo it. The more you interact, the more likely he will want to come out. Just keep things calm and let Fido sleep in this carrier.

Connecting Flights

If your flight is long and has several legs, you may have time in between your flights for Fido to come out of the crate in the airport area. If he has been confined for some time, the first order of business will be to give him an opportunity to relieve himself. Many airports have dog walking areas. However, going to the dog area usually requires you to leave the secure gate area and to go back through security later. This may not be feasible if you have only a little time between connections.

We found it is very beneficial to piddle pad train our small dog, Heidi. This allows Birgit to let Heidi do her business in a public restroom on the pad, which can then be disposed off in the garbage, much like a human diaper. When you travel by airplane, it allows you to stay within the secured area with your dog. Refer back to chapter 5 on specifics about training your dog to potty on command.

Dogs Traveling in the Cargo Hold

If it is your first time flying with your dog, the thought of your dog flying in the cargo hold of the airplane can be a bit unsettling. It may be comforting to know that there are millions of dogs transported by aircraft every week. Birgit brought her collie with her from Germany when she first moved to the United States. She was very nervous and worried about him for the entire 9-hour flight. Akbar was fine, and Birgit will never forget getting him and his crate at the Charlotte Airport. He had been off the flight for 2 hours, patiently waiting in his crate, as Birgit had to go through the long lines at the immigration desk. When she finally got to baggage claim, she was so excited and relieved to see him that she called out his name from across the baggage area. The whole kennel was shaking, as Akbar was excitedly wagging his whole body to greet her.

Every airline has different procedures for dealing with pets, but those that transport them, do so on a regular basis and are well equipped to take care of your precious pet. All will require that you have an IATA (International Air Transport Association) approved hard case sky kennel. There are also strict guidelines on the size of kennel for each dog. To measure your dog and make sure you purchase the correct size crate for him, follow the guidelines on the airline's website. We have decided not to include a sizing guide here, as we have noticed that different airlines had different requirements on their sizing. The best source of information about traveling with a particular airline is their own website. They will have a page specifically for their requirements. You can print out the page and check off each requirement to make sure you have met the requirements. Carefully review your airline's pet policy and ask as many questions as need answering to clarify their guidelines. Once you know what size of crate your dog will need, you can purchase it at a local store or online. Most Airlines will require that the crate is secured by wing nuts and screws, so be sure not to buy a crate that uses snaps. Carriers with snaps might open during travel and you definitely do not want that.

You can find our favorite products for travel at ModernCanineServices.com. Look under our product recommendations tab. Make sure you purchase your crate in advance and allow some time to get your dog familiar with it. We recommend you use the training exercises from Chapter 4 to make him comfortable and allow him to sleep in the crate for several nights prior to your flight.

On the travel day, you will need to line the carrier inside with some absorbent material. You can use potty pads, or for a more inexpensive option, line the carrier bottom with news papers. We also recommend to have a dog bed or blanket inside for comfort. Make sure that the dog has used the blanket or bed before, so that there is a familiar smell. Many airlines will require that you have empty water and food dishes with the crate, even though there will be no food or water given to your dog during the scheduled flight. This is for long layovers or in case there is a flight delay. It allows for the airline attendants to offer food or water to your dog in the event the travel is longer then originally planned. You can tape some of your dog's food in a zip-lock bag onto the outside of the carrier. It is a good idea to include a short note with feeding instructions.

Required Labeling

You are required to have information labels attached to your pet carrier for his safety. Do a web search or call your local Pet or Feed store and ask if they have any *CS-345 Labels* or *"Live Animals"* stickers. Tell them they go on your dog's crate for Airline shipping.

Federal regulations require that each crate is properly labeled with the words *"LIVE ANIMAL"* on the top and at least one side of the crate in 1-inch (2.5 cm) letters. The crate must also have orientation labels. Indicate the top with arrows or *"This End Up"* on at least two sides.

In addition label the crate with your dog's name and your contact information. Be sure to put your mobile number, not your home phone, on the crate. Add a phone number and address of an emergency contact, in case you cannot be reached.

While the cargo area is climate-controlled, temperatures can and do vary. Therefore airlines may disallow pets traveling in the cargo hold during extreme cold or hot weather conditions. Take this into consideration when you plan your trip.

You don't have to worry about air pressure. Every compartment of every plane is pressurized for safety. If your dog is particularly sensitive to temperature or has breathing issues, the cargo area may not be safe. Pets that are brachycephalic - those with short muzzles and flat "snub noses," such as boxers, pugs, and bulldogs - are more susceptible to breathing problems. These breeds have a harder time adjusting to air pressure changes during flight. If you choose to fly with your snub-nosed pet, check with your airline, as some have banned brachycephalic pets completely from commercial flights.

It is important not to feed your dog in the two hours prior to departure, as a full stomach can cause discomfort for a traveling pet.

The airline will want to see your vaccine records and any additional paperwork required for traveling outside of the US. Be aware that in some countries bringing Fido may include a quarantine for your dog. If your flight has layovers, you will want to find out how the pet will be taken care off at the staging area between flights. We highly recommend to find the flight with the fewest legs, so there are less chances of your dog getting left at a baggage area or not being put on the same flight as you are.

Upon arrival at your final destination, you will usually pick up your dog in the over-sized baggage area, but it is a good idea to check with your airline upon check-in to clarify this procedure.

Your Dog Flies WITHOUT You.

Make sure you ask: "*Will my pet be traveling on the same plane as I am?*"

This might seem like a silly question. However, the flight you are taking might not be equipped for live animals. The airline might put you and your dog on different flights.

Don't assume that when you travel with your dog, he must travel at the same time as you do. Sometimes having your dog travel to your destination before you arrive is a good option. You might be taking a multiple stop flight that would be too long for your dog. Or it might be too hectic to get to the airport and get your dog situated, with children to deal with as well.

You can put your dog, by himself, on a flight to your destination and have someone at the other end pick him up. Often times you can find a better flight for your dog then you can for your dog and people. If you do not have someone that can go to the airport and pick up your dog for you, there are companies that will pick up your dog for you.

One option is to find a full-service boarding kennel at the location that you are flying to. Many offer an airport pickup service. For a fee, they will go to the airport and pick up your pet on your behalf and take your pet back to the boarding kennel until you get there.

Another option is a local pet sitting service, many will offer transportation for dogs. Research the internet for pet services and call around to find the right service to get your pet pick-up at the destination airport. Now all you have to do is fly to your destination, go pick up your pet, and start your vacation.

Chapter 16

Travel by Train

If you are considering traveling with your dog on a passenger train, your dog must accompany you in the coach compartment only. At the time of writing this book, US trains have strict regulations on traveling dogs, if they are not service dogs. There is no baggage area where your dog can travel, so the maximum weight dog you are allowed to take with you on a train in the United States is 20 pounds. Your dog must be in a carrier throughout the trip, with a maximum travel time of 7 hours. Since your carrier has to fit underneath the seat, the maximum size of your carrier can be 19 inches long by 14 inches wide by 10 and a half inches high.

US trains require a reservation for your pet, and availability is on a first-come-first-serve basis. Only one pet per person is allowed and no more than five reservations per train. You can not check in with your pet later than 30 minutes before the train leaves so that the ticket agent can confirm the eligibility of your pet. If you are at an unstaffed location, the conductor will evaluate the availability of your pet and give you a waiver form to complete for each leg of travel.

Your dog must be comfortable traveling in a crate. Please refer to Chapter 4 on crate training to make sure your dog is familiar with the crate and comfortable being in it for a longer period of time.

You will want to research the guidelines of the Department of Transportation when traveling with live animals.

If you happen to travel outside the United States, you may find countries that have more dog-friendly options when it comes to traveling by train. Many European trains allow dogs to accompany their owners. It is a good idea to research the specific pet regulations prior to your travel time.

City Public Transportation

Every municipality is different, and policies change frequently for non-service dogs on city public transportation such as light rails, cable cars, or subways. You will need to research online or call ahead.

In most cases where dogs are allowed, they must be in a pet carrier, or, if leashed dogs are permitted, they may be required to wear a muzzle.

If you plan to take your dog on a train, subway or other public transportation, it is a good idea to get him accustomed to moving sidewalks, elevators and other unusual surfaces. You can refer back to the Hometown Adventure Exercises from Chapter 7 to prepare your dog for traveling in Public Transit.

Chapter 17

Resources for Training

Training your dog with the help of our book, or any other dog training guide can be fun and rewarding. It creates a special bond with your canine friend. Having a well-behaved dog makes travel so much more fun. Training can also help your dog stay active and balanced. There are several choices you have to continue working with your dog and to take him further in his training. We would like to point you towards other opportunities that can be fun and helpful in regards to making your dog the perfect pooch.

For a little bit more guidance, you can go to a group class that local pet-food stores offer at a reasonable price. They usually have a multi-week class scheduled. You and your dog can learn some basic obedience once a week. We recommend these types of classes because they help you understand how much control you have over your dog when you get into the public situation. Before going to group class, make sure that your dog's vaccinations are up to date. If after taking your dog to the group class, you feel that your dog is not trained enough, do not feel bad. These group classes will work with only the most behaved and calm dogs.

Another method is one-on-one training. This type of training will be with you, your dog and a professional dog trainer. A professional trainer is able to evaluate you and your dog. He can teach both of you at the same time. We would recommend this type of training if your dog displays behavior problems that you have been unable to work through on your own, or if you would like to work on some advanced obedience with your dog.

You can also take your dog to a trainer for in kennel training. This training is very good when you are limited on time but you still want to have your dog professionally trained. At the end of the training, you should get a few sessions to teach you how to give the commands to your dog and what to expect from your dog.

You and your dog may also enjoy specialty dog sports that bring out your dogs abilities and allow him to exercise and learn. There are many choices, and it depends on your dog's aptitude towards certain behaviors; examples are herding classes, agility, fly ball or water-dogs. Check your local area to find out about dog sporting clubs or groups.

After Words

We hope that you and your dog will enjoy many adventures together. We would love to hear about them. Please join our Facebook group *"Keep Your Paws on the Road"* and share your pictures and stories with our growing community of dog-loving travelers! You can find a link to the Facebook group on our website homepage. You can also find new training videos and blog articles frequently and follow our book tour and event dates.

ModernCanineServices.com

About the Authors

Jim and Birgit Walker

Jim Walker graduated from Sun Valley Dog Training Academy in 1984 and has been training dogs in Arizona, California and Hawaii. His grandfather, Woods Walker, created the renowned Walker Hound breed. Today, Jim's residence is in Phoenix, Arizona. He travels with his wife, Birgit, and their three dogs, Heidi, Jaeger, and Apollo, throughout the United States.

Birgit Walker grew up in Germany. Her family enjoyed hiking vacations with their dogs. Birgit came to the United States in 1989 with her collie, Akbar. She is a certified Yoga and Meditation Instructor, writes a blog and newsletter for Modern Canine Services, and trains dogs with Jim.

Other Books by Birgit Walker

Coming soon

AZ Dog-Friendly Places – A Guide to Arizona
Restaurants that welcome dogs!

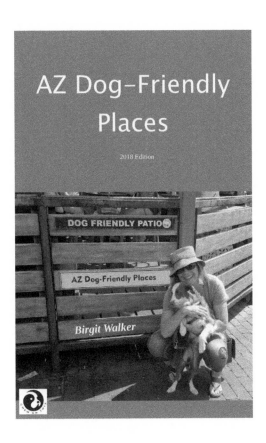

CPSIA information can be obtained
at www.ICGtesting.com
Printed in the USA
FSHW011935171218
54542FS